P9-ARD-381

KAFFE
FASSETT'S
PATTERN LIBRARY

KAFFE FASSETT'S
PATTERN LIBRARY

over 190 creative knitwear designs

The Taunton Press

Dedicated to my impeccable editor and friend Sally Harding
who gave me the idea to do this book

1 3 5 7 9 10 8 6 4 2

Text and knitting designs copyright © Kaffe Fassett 2003
Photography pages 2, 3, 10, 11, 56, 57, 80, 146 copyright © Debbie Patterson 2003
All other photography copyright © Jon Stewart 2003

Kaffe Fassett has asserted his right to be identified as the author of this work under
the Copyright, Designs and Patents Act 1988.

The knitting designs in this book are copyright and must not be produced for resale.

All rights reserved. No part of this publication may be reproduced, stored in a
retrieval system, or transmitted in any form or by any means, electronic, mechanical,
photocopying, recording or otherwise without the prior permission of the copyright
owners.

The Taunton Press
Inspiration for hands-on living®

The Taunton Press, Inc
63 South Main St., PO Box 5506
Newtown, CT 06470-5506
www.taunton.com

First published in the United Kingdom in 2003 by Ebury Press, Random House
20 Vauxhall Bridge Road, London SW1V 2SA

Editor Sally Harding
Art Director Christine Wood
Knitting flat-shot photography Jon Stewart
Special still-life photography Debbie Patterson
Proofreader Claire Wedderburn-Maxwell
Knitting chart illustrations Sally Harding
Techniques illustrations Sally Holmes

ISBN 1-56158-663-3

Printed and bound in Singapore by Tien Wah Press

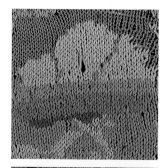

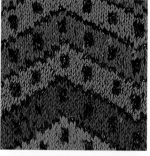

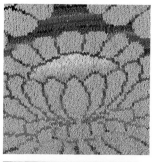

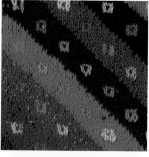

contents

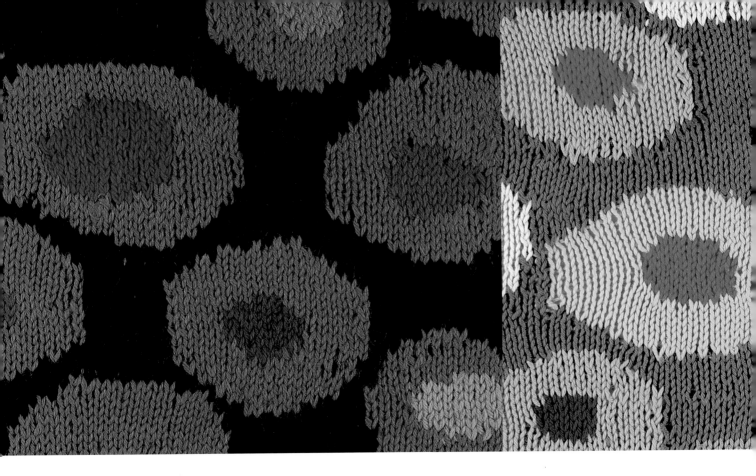

introduction

Books on collections of decorative items are my passion – fans, garden gates, tea pots and, above all, textiles catch my attention. They have me returning again and again to leaf through volumes and marvel at the endless varieties the human eye and hand have achieved. I constantly pour over sample books of weaving, paisley prints and embroidered ribbons. Now, after years of designing knit patterns, I am delighted to present my own collection book of knitted patterns and motifs. They are drawn from swatches I have made while creating designs for the Italian fashion house Missoni, the London-based fashion designer Bill Gibb, Rowan Yarns, private clients, theatre productions and, most recently, the fabulous Peruvian Connection mail-order knit catalogue. Many of these swatch ideas became elements in my final designs and others are appearing here for the first time.

how to use this book

This book is separated into three sections – illustrations of the knitted swatches numbered from 1 to 195; the charts; and tips for using the designs. Beginning with simple stripes, the first chapter is packed with geometric designs based on stripes, squares, crosses, patches, triangles, diamonds, stars and circles. The second chapter is a broad selection of my many figurative motifs and patterns, and features houses, creatures, pots, fruit, foliage and flowers. Simple charts for all the swatches are given in the third chapter. Pass on to the fourth, and final, chapter for practical tips on how to use the charts for your own knits, choose colour palettes and knit with lots of colours.

creating your own designs

As a practising artist, I first started knitting back in the late 1960's when there were precious few knit patterns to emulate, save for traditional Fair Isle, limited to two colours a row, and the ubiquitous argyle. My intricate pattern-on-pattern, still-life paintings contained old prints, embroideries, Oriental carpets and South American stripes, to name but a few. I wanted to tap into this rich source of pattern and colour, as well as into the mosaics, glass, porcelain and ancient textiles on view in European museums like the Victoria and Albert in London. There seemed no reason why this simple craft of knitting couldn't portray all these wondrously beautiful worlds. Suddenly everything I saw became a possible knit pattern – Lavenham's half-timbered Elizabethan houses, mosaics, tiles, formal gardens, even traffic cones on the highway.

Like a magpie, I've kept most of my swatches and colour experiments from my early flights of fancy. What thrilled me in those experiments was how such a simple charted pattern could be translated into something light and fine or bulky and oversized by just changing the needle and yarn size. Or, even more amazing was how the slightest changes of colour and contrast could produce such vastly different effects.

With this flexibility in mind, I decided not to limit any design in this book to a specific yarn or needle size, or even a garment shape. I present you instead with a treasure trove of charted patterns that could end up, in your imaginative hands, as large-scale opera coats or blankets (I've even knitted a set of curtains), or scaled down to create miniature doll's garments and accessories worked on the thinnest needles with the finest thread-like yarns.

And colours! The magic element in any knitted garment or soft furnishing is the colour scheme you bring to it – from the darkest of broody moods through to delicate faded pastels. The colours in the swatches in my collection are just a starting point. It's up to you to ring the changes and use the pattern charts to experiment for yourself. My three different colourways of a bold circular pattern inspired by Austrian painter Gustav Klimpt are good examples of using colour to different effect (see pages 6 and 7). Two of the schemes are spring and summery in mood and the third has a dark winter feel with its purple discs on black. From this you can expand the possibilities by going on to try out different yarn textures and weights.

putting the collection together

Finding all these old motifs has been a fabulous voyage of reminiscence, getting out the large storage bins of swatches I've kept since the early 70's and pouring through them. Memories of working with the Scottish designer Bill Gibb came flooding back. The knit designs I did for his fashion house were my first foray into knitting. I had just learned to knit on a train returning from a trip to a mill in Inverness to buy tweeds for Bill's upcoming collection. Having caught the knitting bug in an instant, I put this new skill to work doing swatches that combined the patterns Bill was doing for a blouse and the ancient plaid he would use for a long coat or skirt. These designs were then produced by knitting machines, as hand knitting was thought too long-winded and unreliable at the time. How things have changed with companies in South America and China producing some of the best hand knits in the world to great acclaim! Pulling swatch after swatch out of the overflowing boxes of my samples, also

brought back vivid memories of my first designs for Rowan Yarns, my many early commissions for one-off knits for special clients and, above all, the designs I did for my first book with the inspired advice of photographer Steve Lovi, who shot and styled my first four books. Each stitch knit and colour chosen seemed to have left its fond imprint – even the names given to long-forgotten pattern experiments came back to me.

There isn't room to include all my swatch treasures, but the edited-down collection should give you plenty to play with. In the last chapter you'll find masses of ideas for using the charts for your own creations – or for group creations!

the delights of knitting

When I produced my first book *Glorious Knitting* in 1986, I was told 'what a pity that knitting has peaked already'. We then experienced an amazing renaissance of the craft. In fact, I was going to call my book *Renaissance Knitting*. I am equally thrilled that we go to print with this book just as knitting is experiencing a resurgence among the young people of many countries.

Those of you who feel knitting has changed your life, *welcome to the club*. I can think of no better occupation to reveal your own creativity and give you hours of blissful occupation.

Kaffe Fassett

geometric patterns

Geometrics are a godsend to those of you who don't want to be tied to a knitting chart. A lot of the geometric patterns in this chapter are so simple and repetitive that they are easily committed to memory. The inspiration for these stripes, squares, triangles, diamonds, stars and circles are mostly quite primitive, so if you wander a bit from the shapes as portrayed here, you will probably improve on them with your own variations. The main thing is to enjoy the use of colour. Remember, when in doubt, add 20 more!

Also, do play with combinations of the patterns – stars with squares, with steps and diamonds – the way old patchwork quilts let patterns dissolve into one another. Don't be afraid of wasting time experimenting. Why not make a long scarf 'sampler' of all the geometrics one after the other in this chapter, it will give you a taste for what's available and you will end up with a wonderful, wacky scarf.

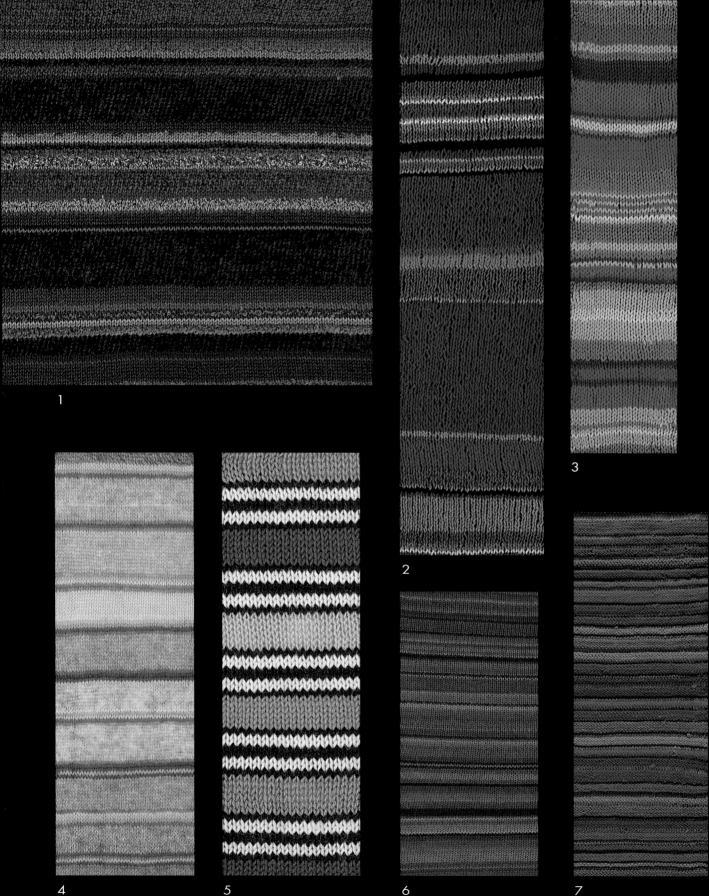

1

2

3

4

5

6

7

8

9

10

11

13

12

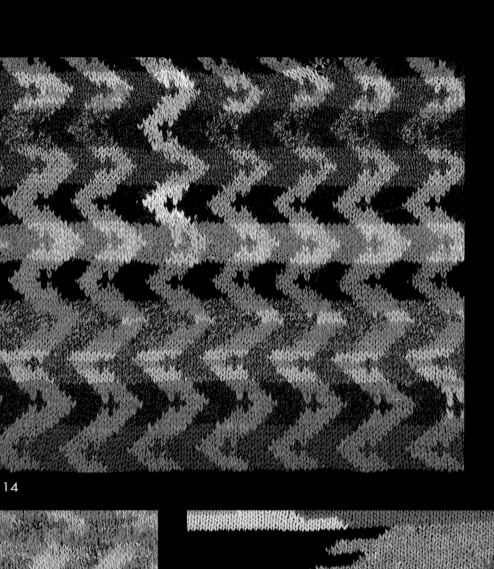

14

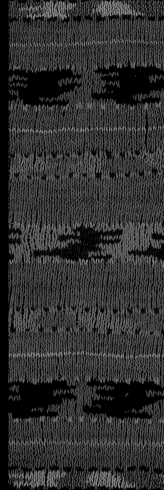

15

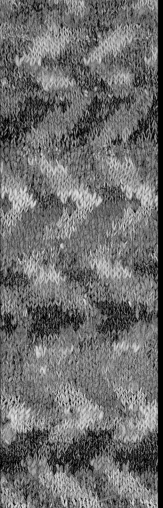

16

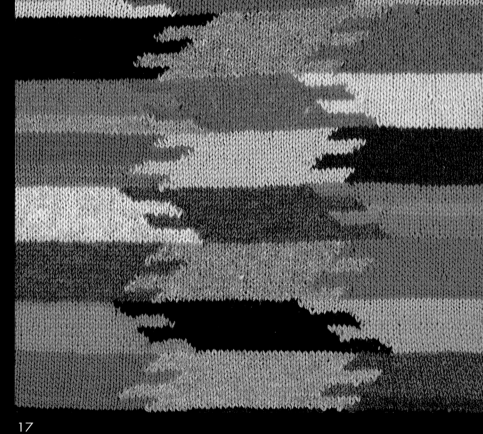

17

18

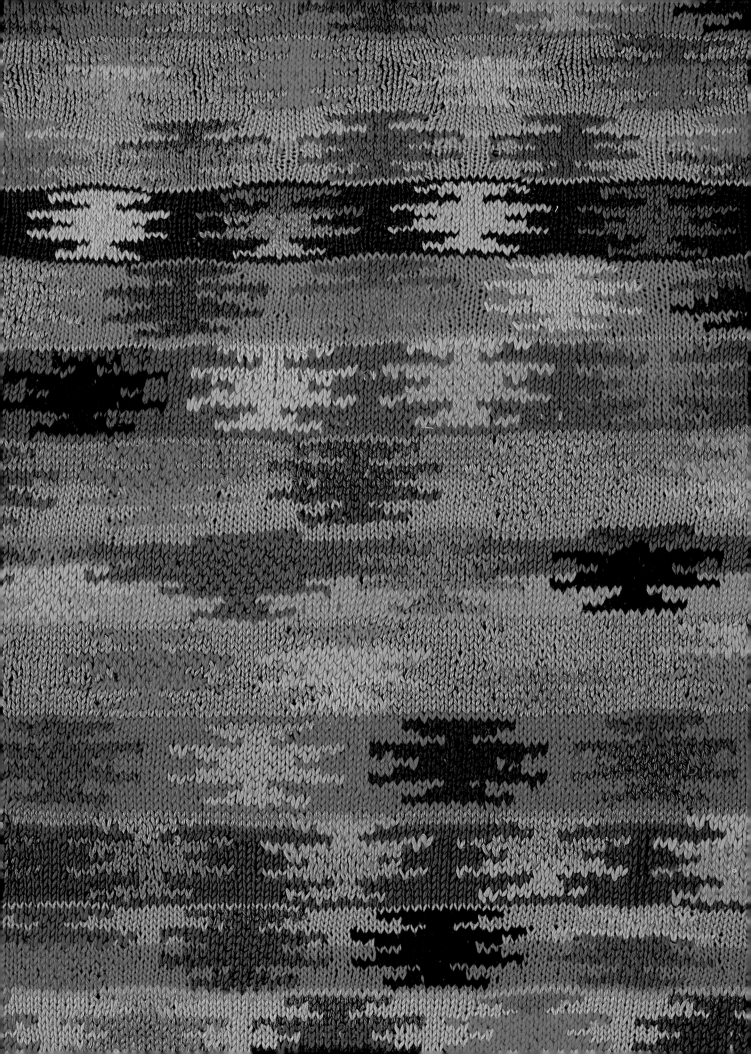

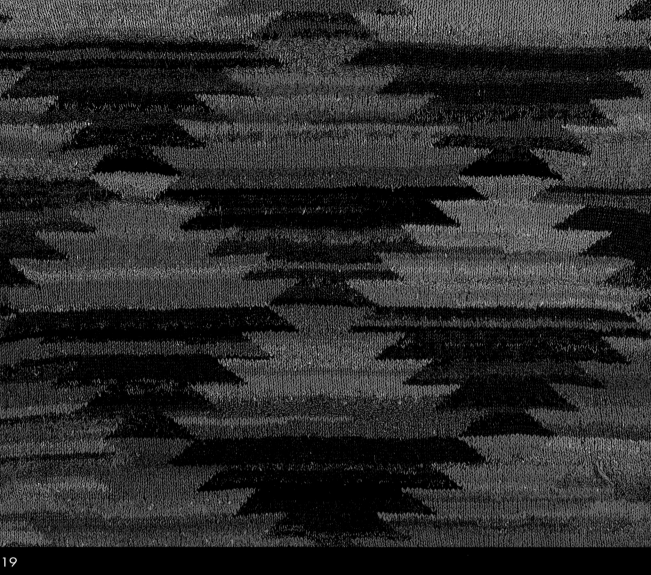

19

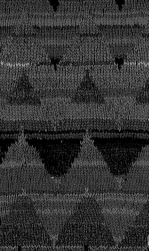

20

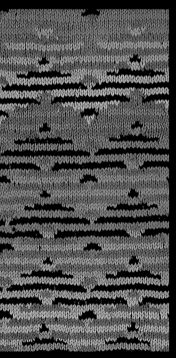

21

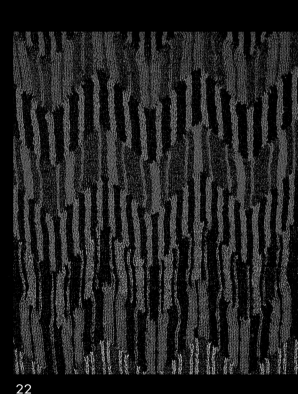

22

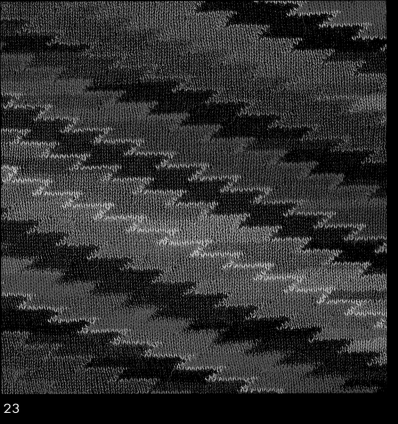

23

24

25

26

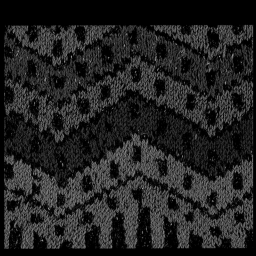

27

28

17

29

30

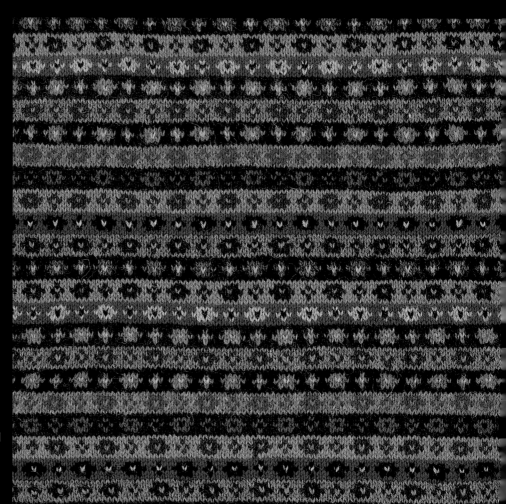

31

32

33

34

35

36

37

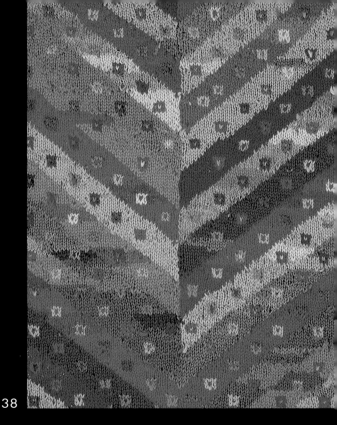

38

39

40

41

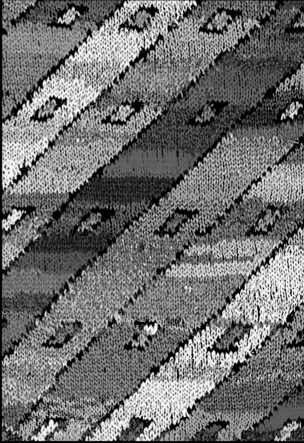

42

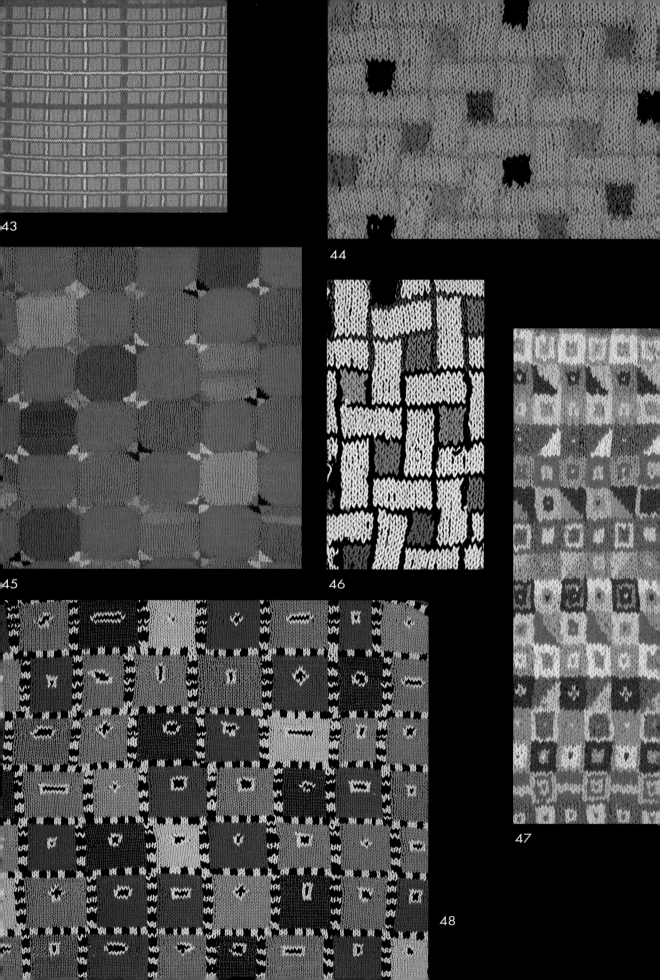

43

44

45

46

47

48

49

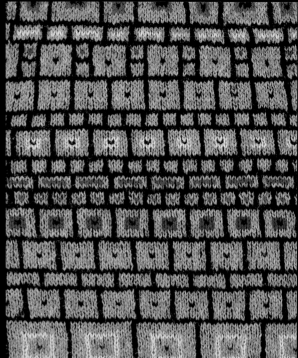

50

51

52

53

54   55

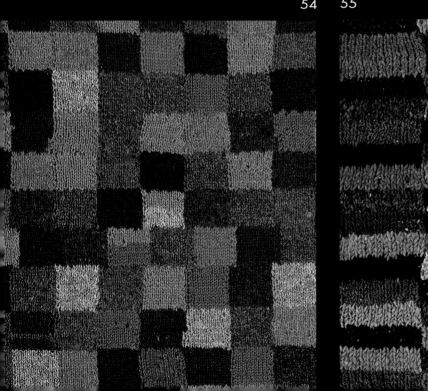

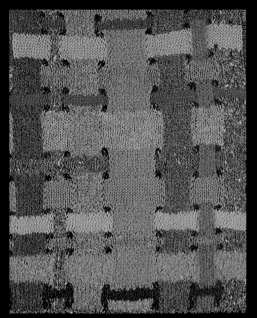
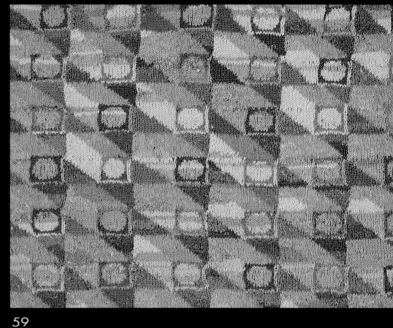

58

59

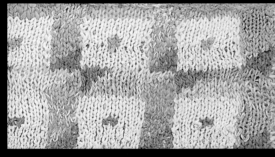
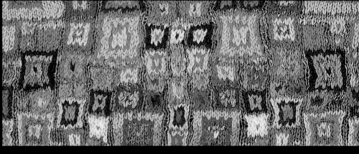

60

61

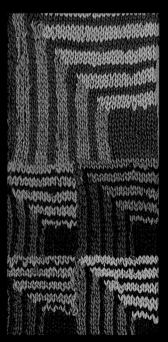

62

63

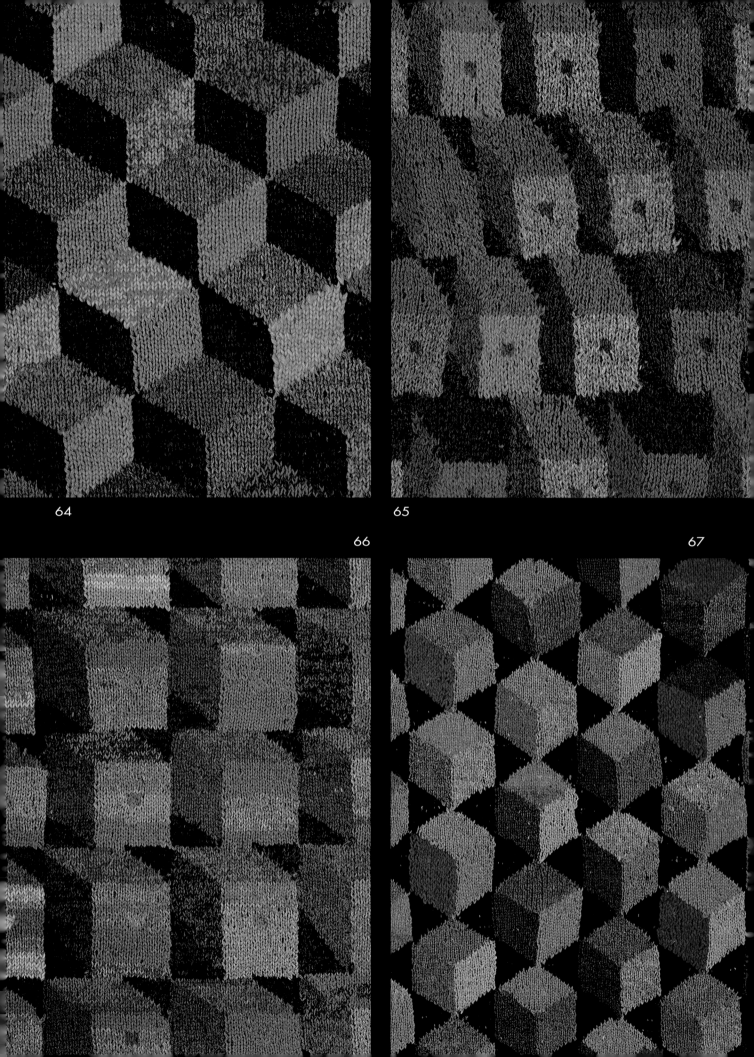

64

65

66

67

68

69

70

71

72

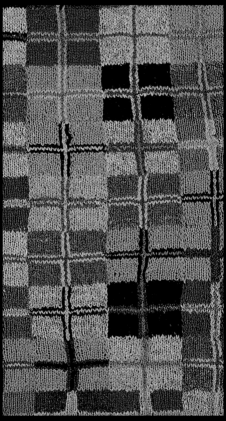

73

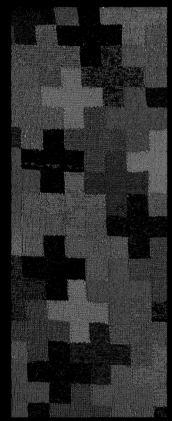

74

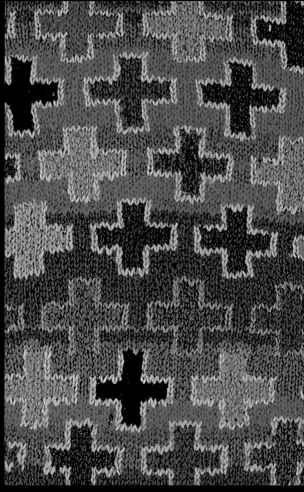

75

76

77

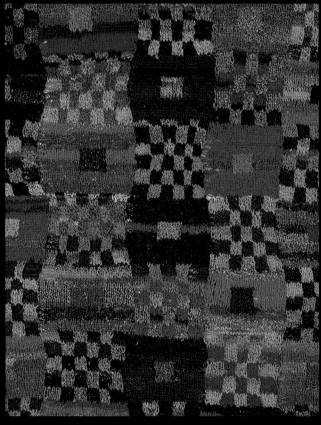

78

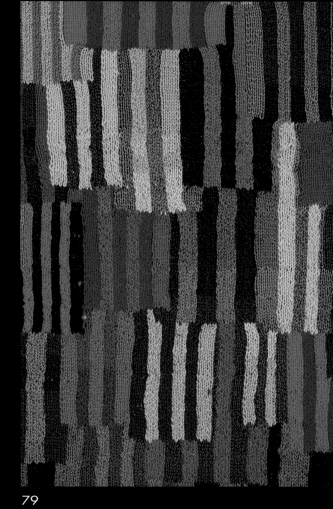

79

80

81

82

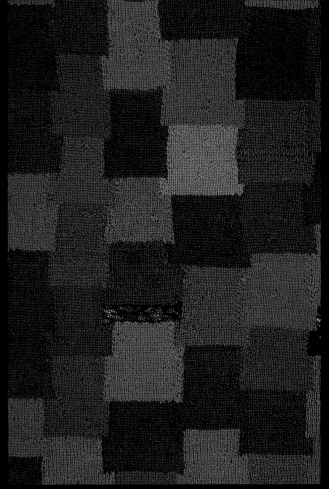

83

84

85

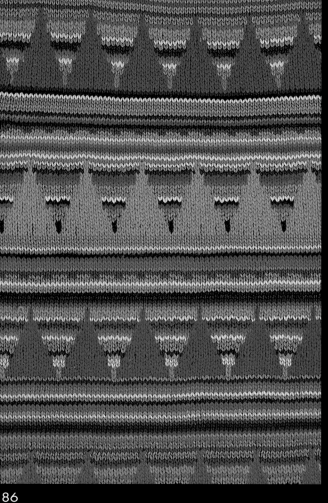

86

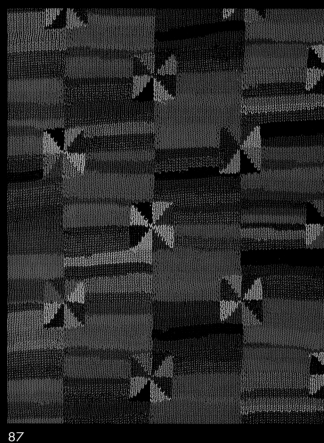

87

88

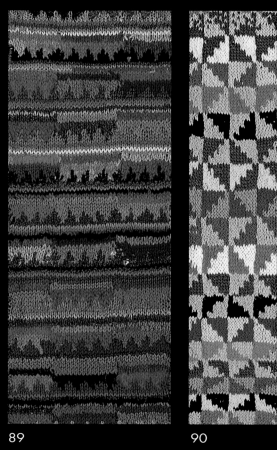

89

90

9

92

93

94

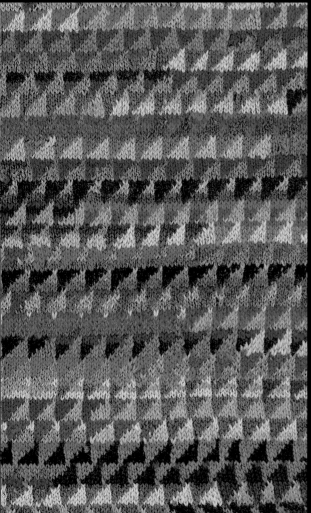

95

96

97

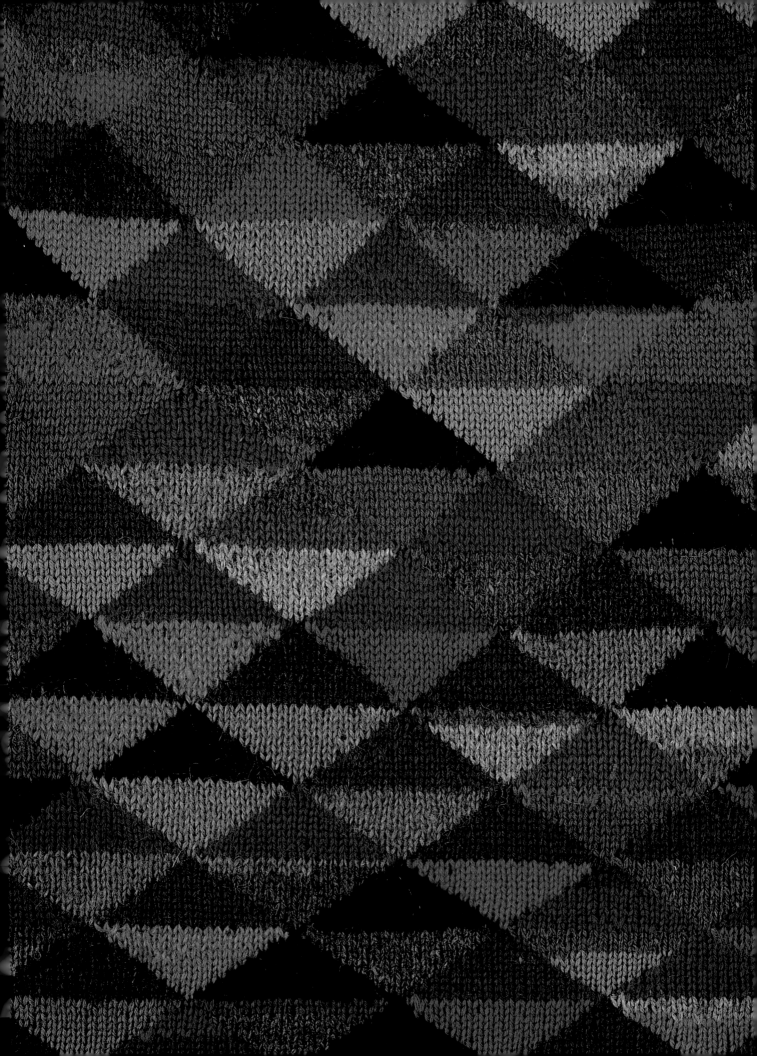

100

101

102

103

104

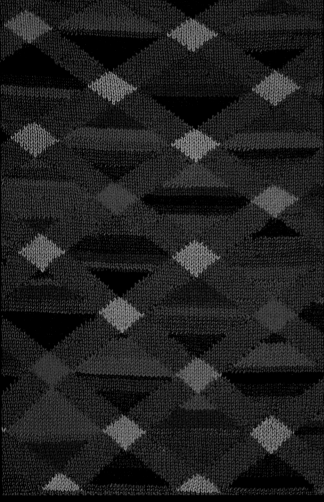

105

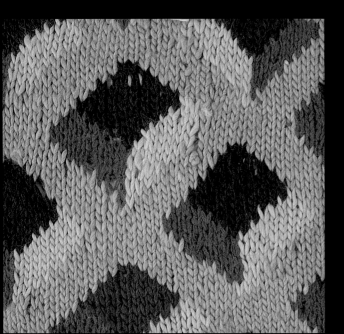

107

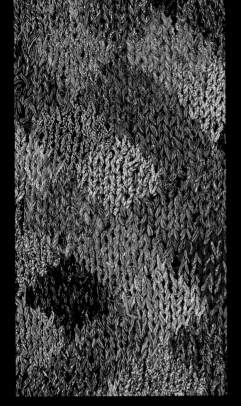

108

109

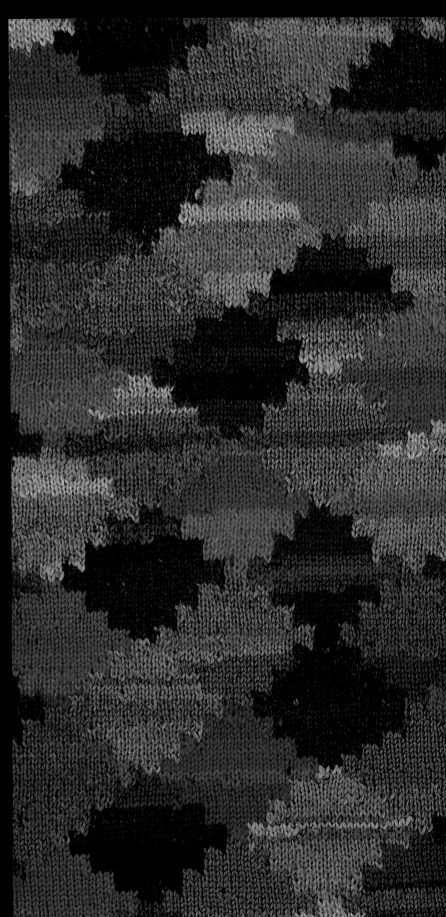

111

112

113

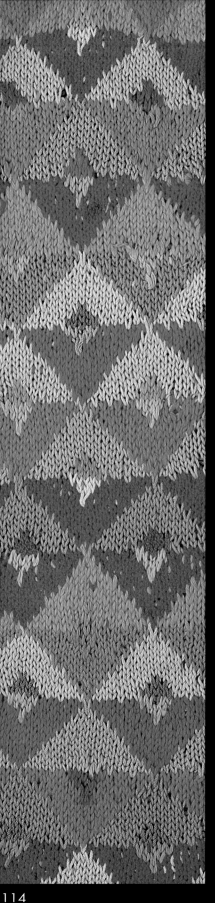

115

114

116

117

118

122

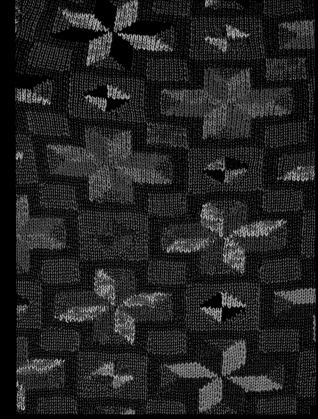

123

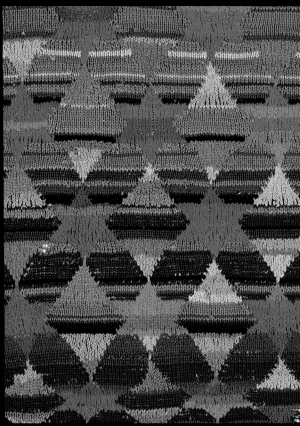

124

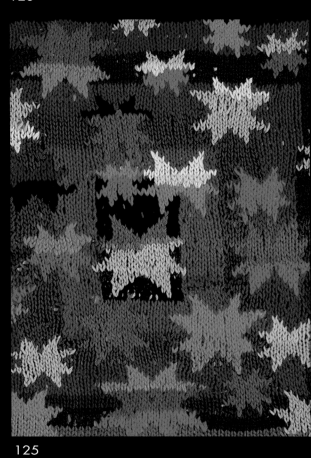

125

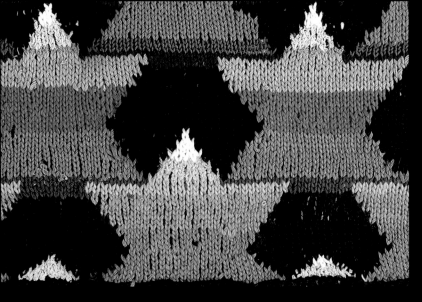

126

127

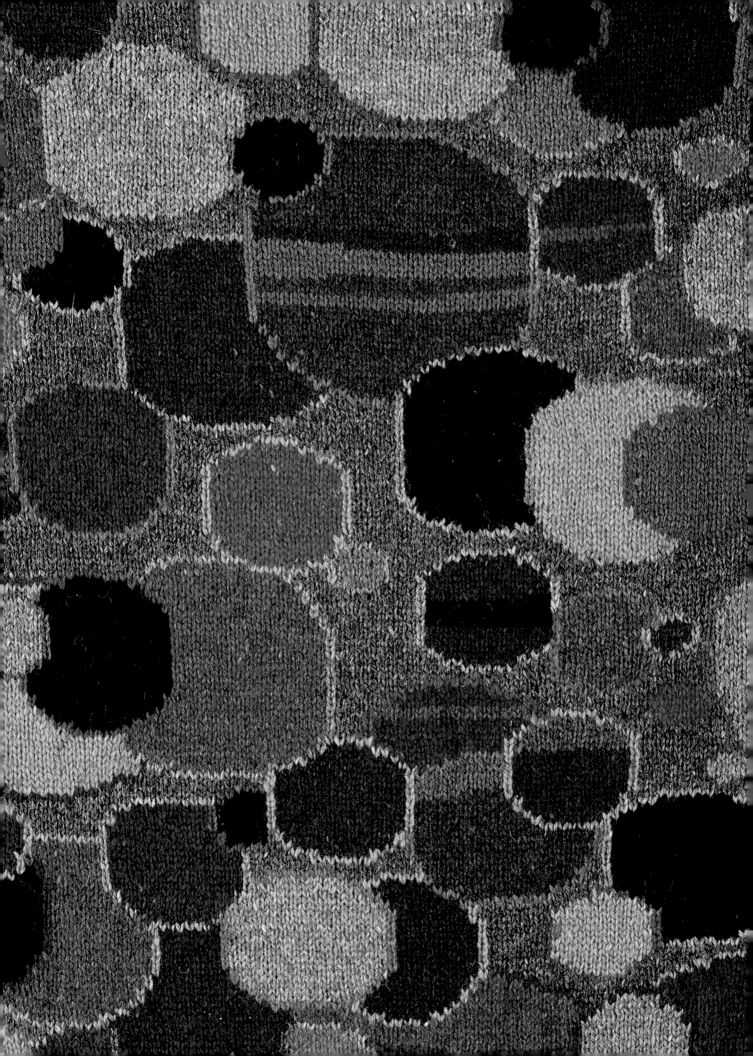

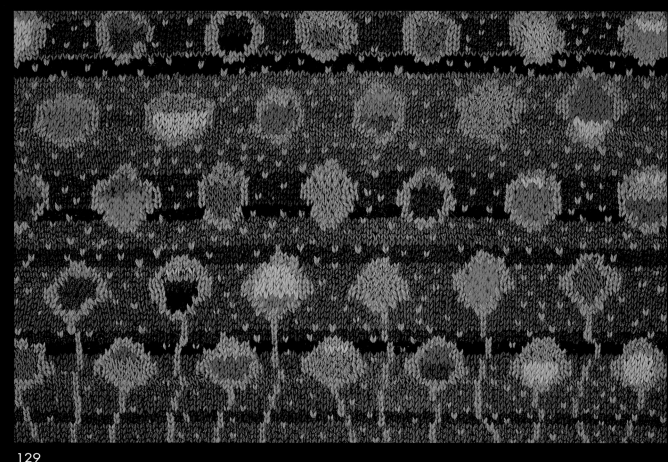

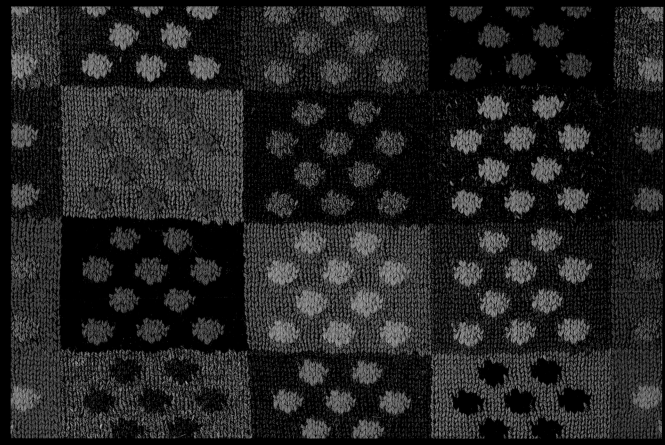

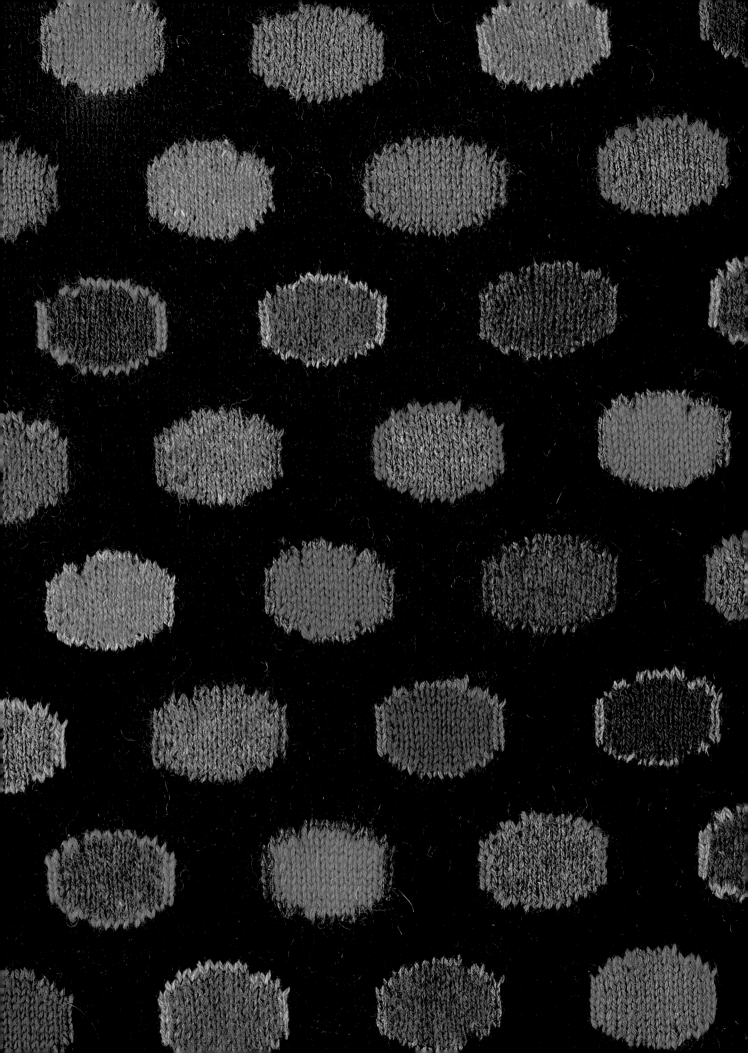

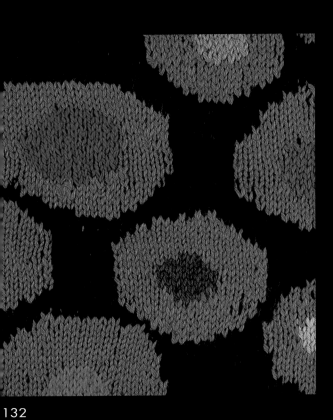

132

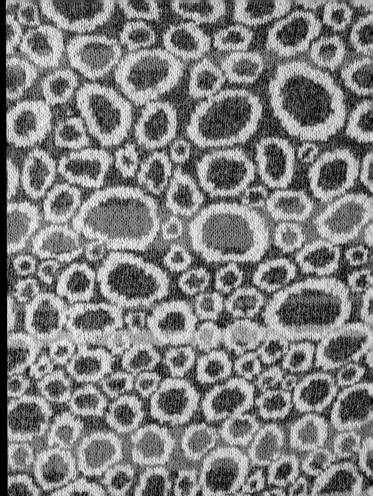

133

134

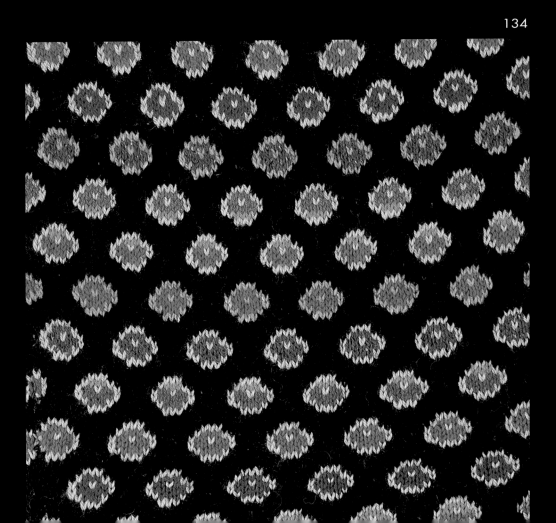

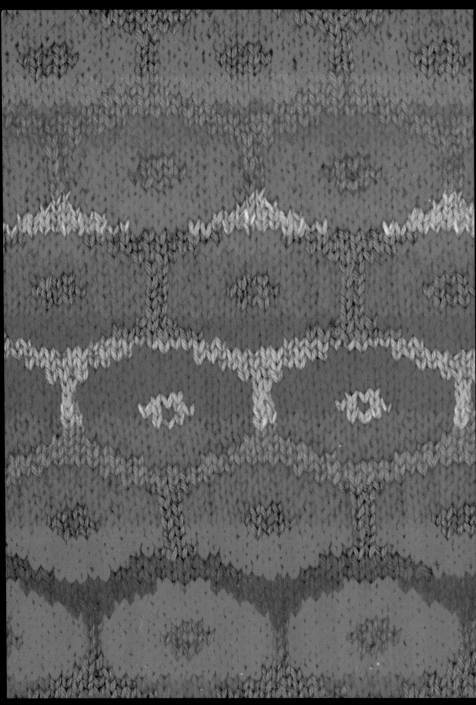

135

136

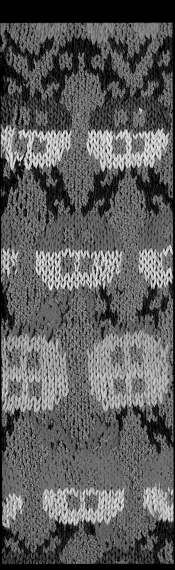

137

figurative patterns

When I first came to the craft I was convinced that only geometric patterns or highly stylized motifs would work on knitting. Researching further, I found that the Victorians knitted highly detailed subjects like flowers, houses and animals on their intricate beaded bags. So, I took the plunge and committed many more subjects to my repertoire. It's amazing how often a flat, two-colours-a-row rendition of a flower or house can come alive on the knitted fabric.

There are still subjects too complex and detailed to read as a knit, but you will find we are hardly limited here with dogs, flowers, fruit, houses and even virgins to choose from. I'm hoping knitters will feel a little frustrated and branch out with subjects of their own. I once did a knit covered with stylized eyes but it hasn't made it to these pages. A male friend of mine did a massively colourful bouquet of flowers in knitting and won a women's magazine contest. So almost anything is possible.

139

140

141

142

143

145

146

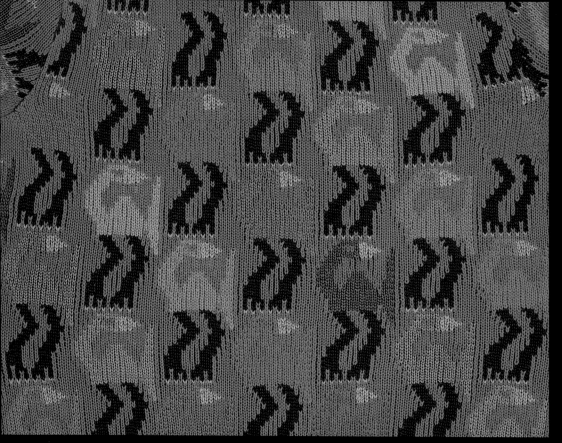

148

150

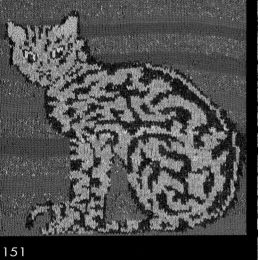

151

152

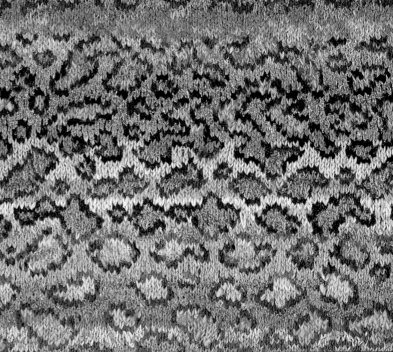

154

155

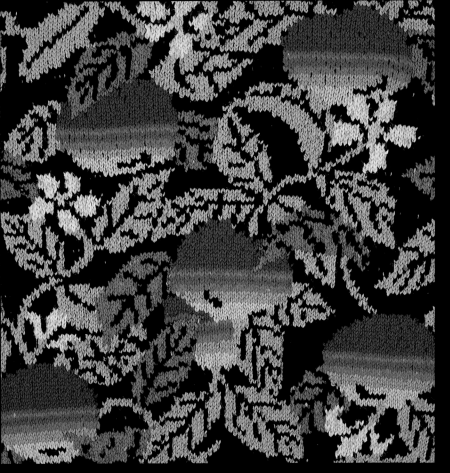

156

157

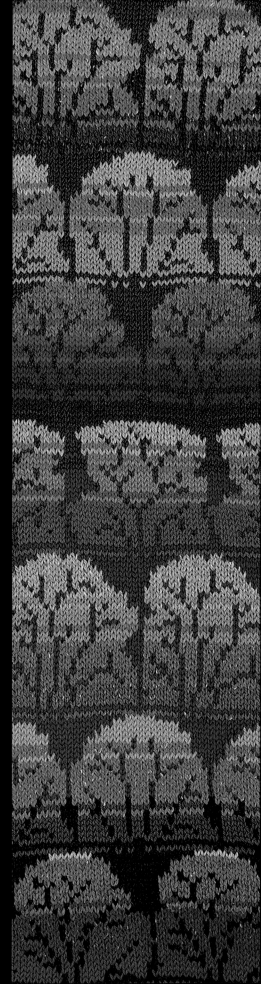

158

159

160

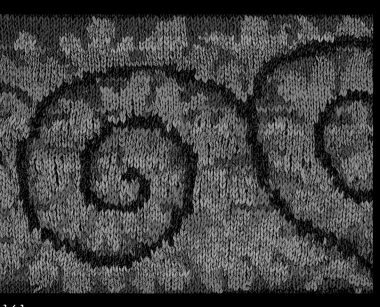

161

162

163

164

165

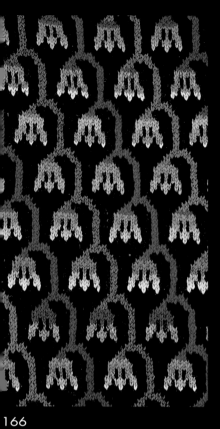

166

168

167

170

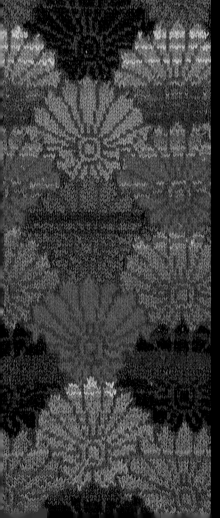

169

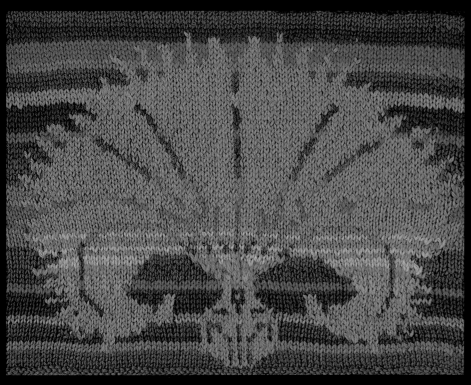

171

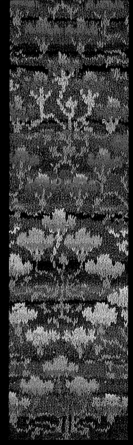

172

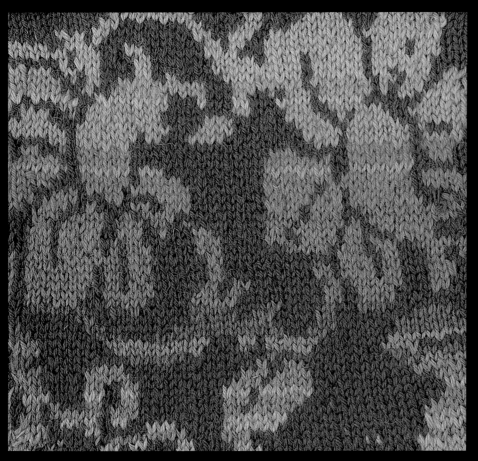

173

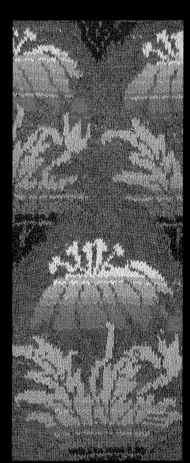

174

75

177

178

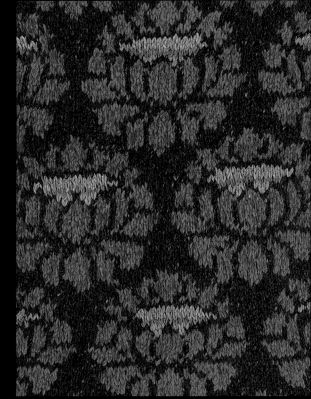

179

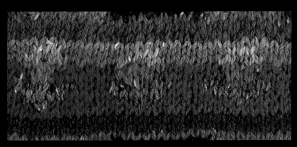

180

181

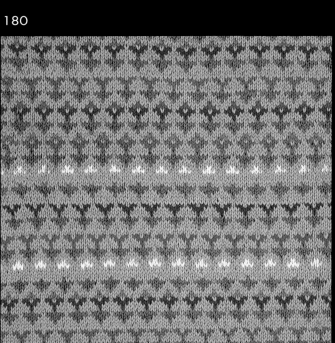

183

184

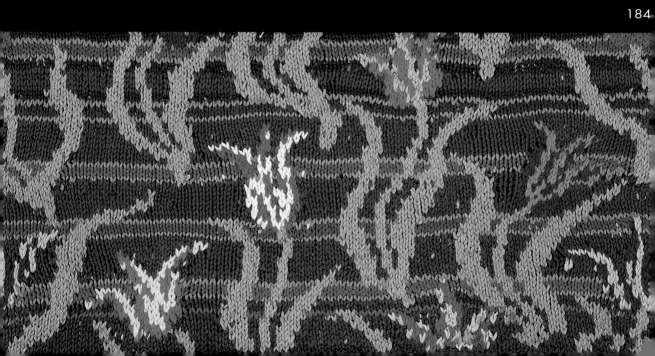

185

186

189

188

191

192

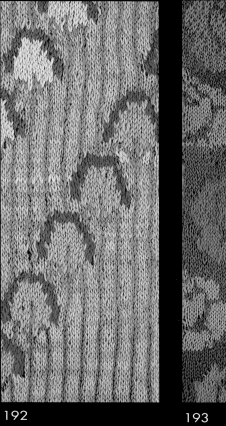

193

194

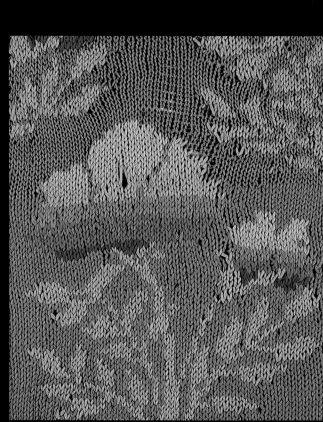

195

knitting charts

This chapter includes charts for the designs in the pattern library on the previous pages. You can find the knitting chart you want by looking for the number given for it in the swatch collection.

Although the swatches sometimes look quite complex, you can see from the simplicity of the charts that most of the designs are actually pretty straightforward. Each square on the chart represents one stitch of knitting, and each horizontal line of squares represents one row of stitches. The symbols represent the coloured shapes of the motifs and patterns. The look of complexity comes from how many colours are introduced into the design. Using lots of colour is not always that hard to do either – you'll find many designs here that are worked using only two colours, for example, in a row of knitting!

Ideas for how to use the designs and the simple techniques for colour knitting are given in the last chapter of the book (see pages 146–157).

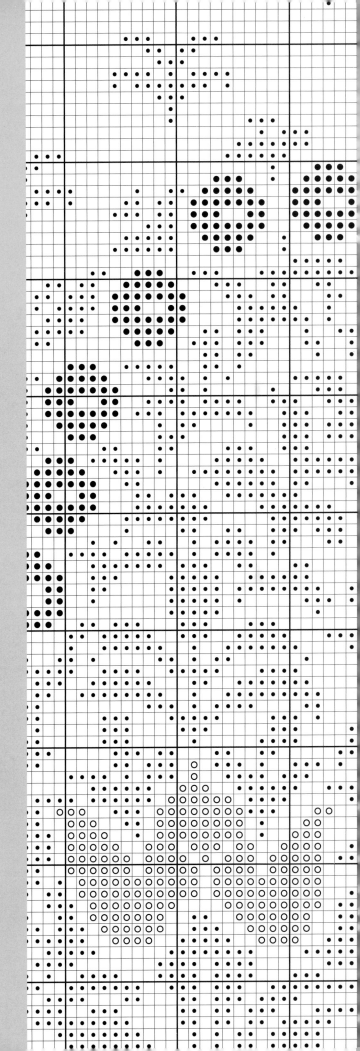

following the charts

These charted knitting patterns show the basic shapes of the patterns and motifs. All of the designs are worked in stocking/stockinette stitch except for Reverse Stocking Stitch Stripe (design no. 7). Different symbols are used to identify the various colour elements in each design. For example, the outline of a shape may be represented with one symbol and the inside of the shape with another, while the background squares remain empty. What colours you use for each shape, and how many colours you use, are up to you. Keeping the charts simple makes them very easy to follow – they provide a pared-down template for you to fill in with your chosen palette. For example, a circular shape or flower shown on the chart as one symbol can be knit up in as many stripes of toning colours as you like. Alternatively, a background can be worked solid or, again, with closely toning shades.

When using the charts, look at the corresponding swatch of the particular motif or pattern in the collection to get an idea of how it will knit up and to spark your ideas for the types of colours to use. Then have a go with your favourite yarns! Some handy tips are given with the charts for how to approach the colouring of the shapes.

motifs and pattern repeats

Most of the charts included are either of a single motif or of a single pattern repeat. To use a pattern repeat, all you do is repeat the number of stitches it takes to make one shape time and again across your row of knitting to get a strip of repeated motifs or patterns; then you repeat the number of rows required for a pattern to make the piece grow as long as you like.

Single motifs can be used in any way you choose – repeated across a piece of knitting or used individually.

partially charted designs

Some of my designs, however, don't break down into neat, small pattern repeats. Instead they are composed of random shapes, for example circles of different sizes and shapes that never repeat over the entire back of a sweater. For these designs, it is not possible to include an entire sweater back, so only a section of the design is given. With this section you can make a small swatch or, with thick yarn, a not-so-small swatch – certainly enough for a square of a patched blanket or even for a cushion front.

These charted sections can also be used as a start for a larger chart that you could draw on graph paper yourself. How the random shapes are built up is easy to see from the section provided.

simple stripes

1 Roman Stripe No. 1 (page 12)
My series of Roman-style stripes were popular in the 40's when my mother was young, and I remember seeing their striking changes of scale on scarves, blouses and furnishings when I was 5 or 6 years old.
Pattern instructions: There is no chart for this design as it is made up of randomly arranged narrow, broad and medium-width stripes. Use the sample for colour combination and yarn texture ideas. Work the design in stocking/stockinette stitch over any number of stitches and vary the number of rows for each stripe.

2 Roman Stripe No. 2 (page 12)
Pattern instructions: There is no chart for this design as it is made up of random stripes. The sample on page 12 is worked in chenille yarns. The stripes have widely different widths – the narrowest is a single row deep and the widest 28 rows deep. Work the design in stocking/stockinette stitch over any number of stitches and vary the number of rows for each stripe.

3 Roman Stripe No. 3 (page 12)
Pattern instructions: There is no chart for this design. Work it in stocking/stockinette stitch over any number of stitches, knitting randomly arranged, narrow contrasting stripes that are one, two, three or five rows deep.

4 Korean Stripe (page 12)
I have always been drawn to this colourful stripe on Korean dance costumes. It's usually worked in brilliant contrasting colours.
Pattern instructions: There is no chart for this design. Work it in stocking/stockinette stitch over any number of stitches, knitting broad eight-row to 10-row stripes in pale neutral shades separated by four or five one-row stripes in random colours.

5 Egyptian Stripe (page 12)
This rather formal stripe can be found on ancient Egyptian caskets in the British Museum in London and in the New York Metropolitan.
Chart note: On the sample swatch of this design on page 12, rows 1–8 are worked in navy and white and the six-row stripe bands are worked in different colours.

6 Peruvian Stripe (page 12)
The multi-tonal intensity of the South American woven stripes that inspired this design is captivating. This knit was designed for the mail-order company Peruvian Connection.
Pattern instructions: There is no chart for this design. Work it in stocking/stockinette stitch over any number of stitches, knitting one-, two-, three- and four-row stripes randomly.

7 Reverse Stocking Stitch Stripe (page 12)
Unusually for me, I used purl stitches on the right side of this knit. It is a good textured knit for a top or scarf, as it drapes deliciously.
Pattern instructions: There is no chart for this design as it is worked in stripes of random widths. Work it over any number of stitches, randomly introducing three-, four-, five- and six-row ridged stripes in reds and pinks, separated by two rows of stocking/stockinette stitch in one-row stripes. To work the ridges, change to the ridge colour and work the first row in stocking/stockinette stitch; then work the remaining two, three, four or five rows in reverse stocking/stockinette stitch.

8 Echo Stripe (page 13)
Chart note: In this swatch the regular · stripes are worked in dark grey and medium grey, with single-row stripes in varying colours running through them.

5 Egyptian Stripe

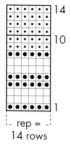

8 Echo Stripe

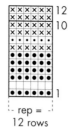

9 Blanket Stripe No. 1

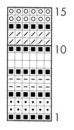

10 Blanket Stripe No. 2

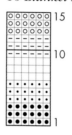

12 Blanket Stripe No. 3

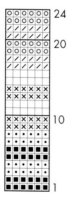

13 Blanket Stripe No. 4

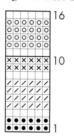

9 Blanket Stripe No. 1 (page 13)
These four simple, regular Blanket Stripes were all worked for a blanket made up of striped patchwork squares (see pages 10 and 11).
Chart note: Choose a single colour for the one-row stripes and vary the colour of the two-row stripes. If you work an even number of rows like this between the single-row stripes you will always arrive back at the right end of the knitting to pick up the dropped single-row colour. Break off and weave in the ends of the two-row stripe yarns (see page 157).

10 Blanket Stripe No. 2 (page 13)
Chart note: Choose your colours and introduce them randomly for these regular three-row stripes.

11 Dress Stripe (page 13)
In the early 80's I knit several dresses with highly patterned square yokes and long draped panels of chenille and wool stripes. Most of them used one background colour with shots of brighter colour running through it.
Pattern instructions: There is no chart for this stocking-/stockinette-stitch design as it is worked in stripes of random widths. Grey stripes one, two, three, four, five and six rows deep are scattered throughout, and other colours are introduced as one-row stripes.

12 Blanket Stripe No. 3 (page 13)
Chart note: To achieve this type of two-row stripe pattern, use one set of two contrasting colours for eight rows, then change to two different colours for the next eight rows, and so on.

13 Blanket Stripe No. 4 (page 13)
Chart note: To unify this stripe pattern, use the same colour for all the one-row stripes, while varying the colours of the two- and four-row stripes. There is no need to break off and weave in the single-row colour – just drop it at the side and pick it up again when it's needed.

zigzag stripes

14 Zigzag (page 14)

An Islamic stone arch showing deep contrasts of dark and light inspired this knit pattern.

Chart note: Work this with only two colours in each row for an easy-to-knit pattern, or work each vertical stripe in intarsia and in a different colour.

15 Ikat Stripe (page 14)

Although perfect for borders, this stripe can also be used as a shot of detail across large plain areas of knit.

Chart note: The four charts for this design can be worked separately or combined to make a long repeating stripe pattern. For the complete stripe pattern, begin with Chart 1. After completing rows 1–29, work the broad stripe over rows 7–19 again, then work Chart 2. Continue like this, working the Chart 3 and 4 stripes with the broad stripe between them.

16 Tall Zigzag (page 14)

Use the chart for no. 14 (Zigzag) for this design.

17 Pale Ikat (page 14)

Chart note: A regular repeat is given for this pattern, but it is so easy to do that you can vary the shapes and depths of the stripes randomly as you knit for a more dynamic design. Choose a different colour for each shape, using the intarsia technique.

18 Mirage (page 15)

This jazzy pattern was inspired by my passion for kilim rugs. I knitted it on my first trip to India – hence the spicy hot palette.

Chart note: Use a different set of colours for each motif. Carry the background colour across the row and work the motifs in intarsia.

14 Zigzag

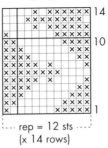

rep = 12 sts
(x 14 rows)

18 Mirage

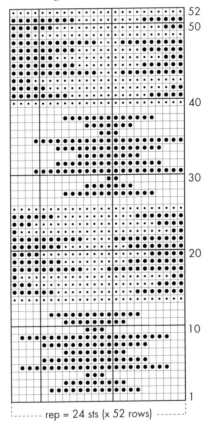

rep = 24 sts (x 52 rows)

15 Ikat Stripe CHART 1

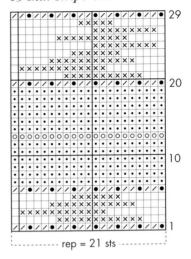

rep = 21 sts

15 Ikat Stripe CHART 2

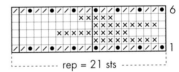

rep = 21 sts

15 Ikat Stripe CHART 3

rep = 21 sts

15 Ikat Stripe CHART 4

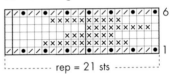

rep = 21 sts

17 Pale Ikat

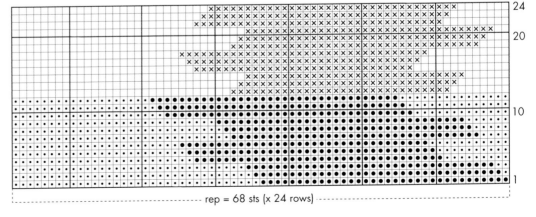

rep = 68 sts (x 24 rows)

19 Earth Carpet

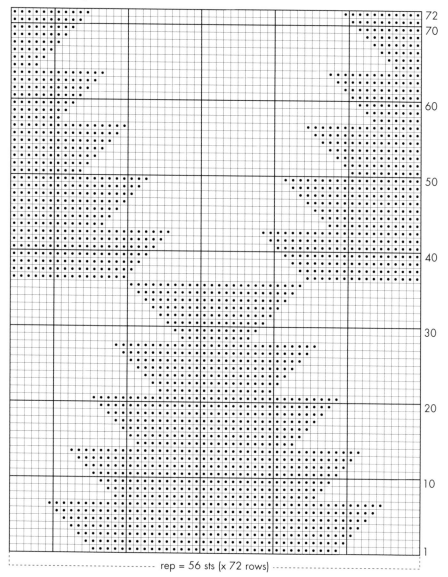

------ rep = 56 sts (x 72 rows) ------

20 Antique Zigzag

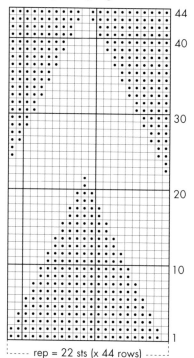

----- rep = 22 sts (x 44 rows) -----

21 Striped Jack's Back

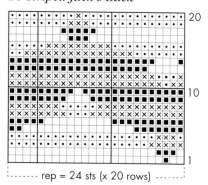

------ rep = 24 sts (x 20 rows) ------

19 Earth Carpet (page 16)

Earth Carpet is one of the most popular designs from my first knitting book, Glorious Knitting. *It is an adaptation of a kilim carpet motif. Working this pattern is a great way to use two groups of colours, one dark and one medium to light. The pattern is deceptively easy and fast to knit, especially on a big scale for a coat or jacket worked in chunky yarns or with several strands used together.*

Chart note: If desired, make the tiered shapes deeper and wider for a larger-scale design.

20 Antique Zigzag (page 16)

Dead easy to knit, this pattern provides an exciting method for streaking light and dark colours across a piece of knitting.

Chart note: Use a different set of tones for each contrasting zigzag. Only two colours are needed in each row, so carry the colour not in use across the back of the work, weaving it in on at least every fifth stitch (see page 156).

21 Striped Jack's Back (page 16)

This interesting stripes-on-stripes version of Jack's Back (design no. 25 on page 17) uses highly contrasted hues.

Chart note: Use bold contrasts for the stripes across this pattern. It requires only two colours in each row.

85

22 Finnish Zigzag (page 16)

Chart note: Five regular vertical stripe patterns fill the zigzags on this design; these do not form an exact repeat so just continue them as set across your knitting. Repeat rows 17–36 to continue the zigzag design and fill each zigzag with a new and different vertical stripe.

23 Lightning (page 17)

Made for a Peruvian Connection collection, this knit came from an ancient Peruvian pattern. It is excellent for showing off many good colours in a single design.

Chart note: The chart provides a simple regular repeat, but you can vary the width of the diagonal zigzags if you like. Each stripe uses a different set of closely toning shades. Vary the outline colours.

23 Lightning

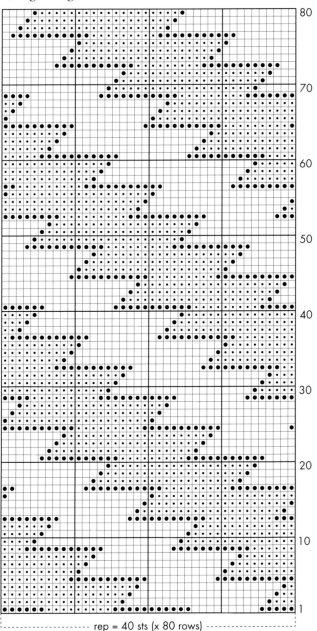

------------ rep = 40 sts (x 80 rows) ------------

22 Finnish Zigzag

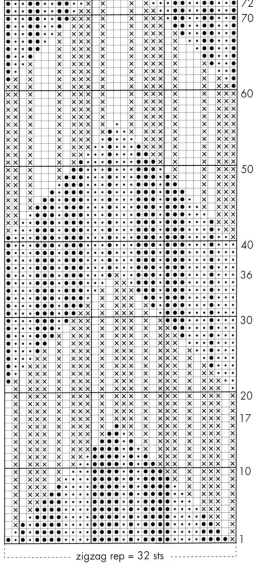

------ zigzag rep = 32 sts ------
x 20 rows (rows 17–36)

24 Sunset

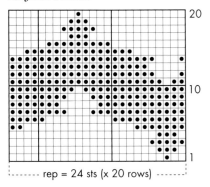

25 Jack's Back

rep = 24 sts (x 20 rows)

26 Foolish Virgin Border Stripe

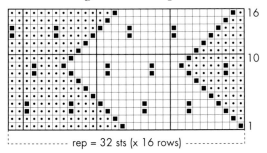

rep = 32 sts (x 16 rows)

24 Sunset (page 17)

An old kilim was the model for this pattern. One knitter worked it entirely in brilliantly coloured ribbons – a smashing result!

Chart note: There is a row repeat for this chart, but no stitch repeat, so use the single repeat across the entire width of your knitting. Add more stitches at each side if you need to make a wider textile. Use one set of contrasting colours for the first 55-row repeat, then change to a new set.

25 Jack's Back (page 17)

I first used this design on the back of a waistcoat/vest for Jack Frances, the great carpet expert at the London auction house Sotheby's, hence the name. As for Zigzag (design no. 14 on page 14), an Islamic arch sparked off the idea for the shape.

Chart note: Work the shapes using only two colours in each row. You can use many toning shades for each stripe.

26 Foolish Virgin Border Stripe (page 17)

An excellent all-over pattern or border, this stripe provided the perfect frame for my Foolish Virgins (see pages 146 and 147, and design no. 146 on page 60). The simple dots sprinkled through the zigzag enliven the design.

Chart note: After completing row 16, begin from row 1 again to work the repeat, but continue working the dots three rows apart, positioning them inside each stripe between the stripe outlines as before (five stitches apart).

mixed stripes

27 Japanese Sock Stripe
(page 17)
I used this vibrant stripe on a Japanese sock design that was never produced. It makes a good border for other designs.
Chart note: Work each zigzag in the design in a different colour for a strong effect.

28 High Contrast Zigzag
(page 17)
Chart note: Work each zigzag with a different colour or try the design using only two colours in each row.

27 Japanese Sock Stripe

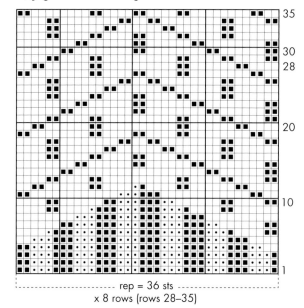

rep = 36 sts
x 8 rows (rows 28–35)

28 High Contrast Zigzag

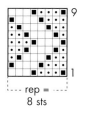

rep = 14 sts
(x 6 rows)

29 Oriental Motifs (page 18)
A waistcoat/vest was covered with this very early design, which I created as a knitting pattern for the Women's Home Industries. You could use it for a deep border on a blanket, the bottom of a coat or a long cuff perhaps.
Chart note: The individual patterns that make up this long mixed stripe have different stitch-repeats, so they are separated into five charts. Use the charts on their own, or combine them, starting with Charts 1–6, then working Charts 5–1 back to the beginning in reverse order, to make up the full pattern.

29 Oriental Motifs CHART 1

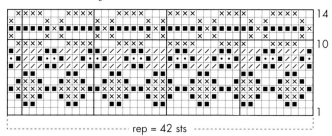

rep = 42 sts

29 Oriental Motifs CHART 2

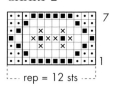

rep = 12 sts

29 Oriental Motifs CHART 3

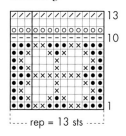

rep = 13 sts

29 Oriental Motifs CHART 4

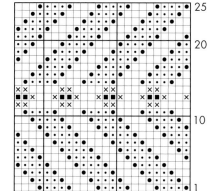

rep = 24 sts

29 Oriental Motifs CHART 5

rep = 7 sts

29 Oriental Motifs CHART 6

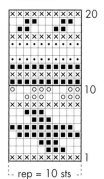

rep = 8 sts

30 Celtic Stripe CHART 1

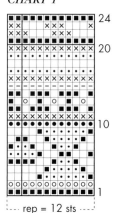

rep = 12 sts

30 Celtic Stripe CHART 2

rep = 10 sts

30 Celtic Stripe (page 18)
Celtic Stripe is the very first Fair Isle pattern I had published. Designed for the Vogue Knitting Book *in the 70's, it has a* Book of Kells *influence and is mostly worked in one or two colours a row, although there are some three-colour rows.*
Chart note: Not all the patterns in this mixed stripe have the same stitch-repeat, so it is divided into two charts. Work Charts 1 and 2 alternately to form the design.

31 Dot Border Stripes

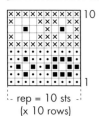

rep = 10 sts
(x 10 rows)

32 Random Lattice Stripe

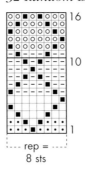

rep =
8 sts

33 Regular Lattice Stripe

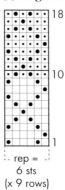

rep =
6 sts
(x 9 rows)

35 Mosaic Stripe

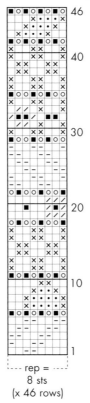

rep =
8 sts
(x 46 rows)

34 Stripes & Crosses

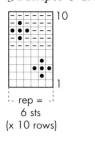

rep =
6 sts
(x 10 rows)

37 Diagonal Box Stripe CHART 1

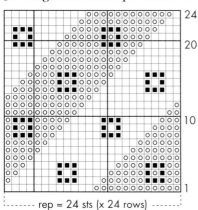

rep = 24 sts (x 24 rows)

37 Diagonal Box Stripe CHART 2

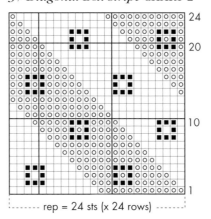

rep = 24 sts (x 24 rows)

31 Dot Border Stripes (page 18)
Here's a neat little stripe that can be as rich in colour as you choose – or done in black, grey and white.
Chart note: Only two rows in this 10-row repeat use three colours; the other rows are either one-colour rows or two-colour rows.

32 Random Lattice Stripe (page 19)
A lattice imposed on bold stripes of blending or contrasting tones helps to harmoniously merge the stripes together.
Chart note: Use the same colour for the lattice throughout and change the stripe colour randomly. Vary the width of the stripes for a different look. With only two colours a row, this is simple colour knitting.

33 Regular Lattice Stripe (page 19)
Chart note: Change the stripe colour and the lattice colour every nine rows. This design uses only two colours a row.

34 Stripes and Crosses (page 19)
Chart note: Change the stripe colour every five rows, but keep the crosses the same colour within the rows to unify the pattern.

35 Mosaic Stripe (page 19)
A simple mixed stripe that is fun to knit, this was another early pattern for Women's Home Industries. It gives a very rich detailed look to your knitted fabric.
Chart note: This pattern is mostly worked with two colours a row.

36 Dot Border Stripes (page 19)
Use the chart for no. 31 (Dot Border Stripes) for this design.

37 Diagonal Box Stripe (page 20)
A great vehicle for colour, bright or subdued. Once you get the diagonal colours going it's a doddle to knit – with dots worked in Fair Isle, and diagonals in intarsia.
Chart note: Use the right- or left-leaning diagonals chart; or work one on one side of your knitting and the other on the other side.

38 Diagonal Box Stripe (page 20)
Use the chart for no. 37 (Diagonal Box Stripe) for this design.

39 Column Dot Stripe (page 20)
I designed this for the back of a waistcoat/vest for the Peruvian Connection mail-order catalogue (the front is design no. 181, Flower Ribbon, as shown on page 155). It was inspired by old paisley-print stripes and would make a very smart all-over pattern for a sleeveless top and matching jacket.

Chart note: Keep the motifs the same colour across all the knitting, but use a different background colour in each vertical column. Work the motifs by stranding the yarn across the row, but use the intarsia method for the stripes.

40 Caucasian Stripe (page 21)
I used plenty of colours to make this formal diagonal a rich layout and kept the little crosses a consistent colour that 'reads' well against the striped tones.

Chart note: Use different toning shades for each diagonal. The crosses don't form part of the row-repeat, so after you have worked row 22, continue positioning the crosses inside the diagonal stripes as shown on rows 1–22.

41 Temple Steps (page 21)
An ancient Peruvian weaving I saw inspired this Peruvian Connection design.

Chart note: Work each diagonal stripe in two contrasting sets of toning colours.

42 Nomad Diagonals (page 21)
You can make diagonal stripes bolder by knitting them wider like this. Nomad Diagonals features on a deeply fringed shawl (page 151).

Chart note: Use a dark colour for the one-stitch stripes between the diagonals and the outlines around the little parallelograms.

39 Column Dot Stripe

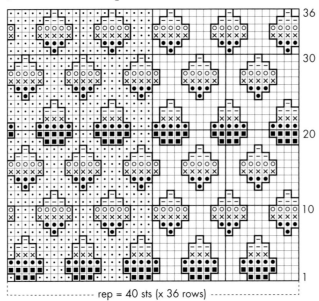

rep = 40 sts (x 36 rows)

40 Caucasian Stripe

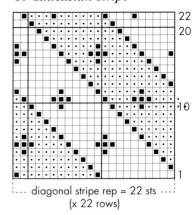

diagonal stripe rep = 22 sts
(x 22 rows)

41 Temple Steps

42 Nomad Diagonals

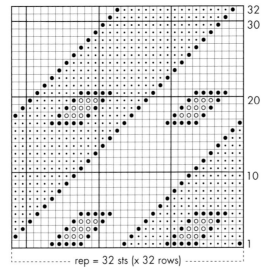

rep = 32 sts (x 32 rows)

rep = 36 sts (x 72 rows)

90

43 Plaid

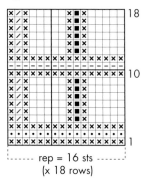

```
          18
          10
```

rep = 16 sts
(x 18 rows)

47 Little Boxes

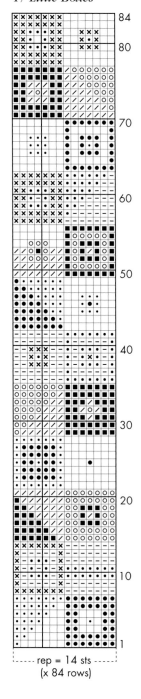

```
84
80
70
60
50
40
30
20
10
1
```

rep = 14 sts
(x 84 rows)

45 Fancy Chequerboard

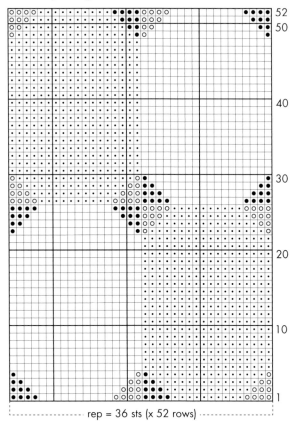

```
52
50
40
30
20
10
1
```

rep = 36 sts (x 52 rows)

46 Woven Tile

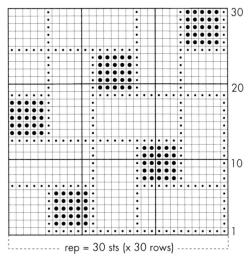

```
30
20
10
1
```

rep = 30 sts (x 30 rows)

squares

43 Plaid (page 22)
All plaids are effective in knitting, but this simple one is easy and graphic.

Chart note: Work the centres of the horizontal and vertical stripes in varying colours, using the intarsia technique for the vertical ones.

44 Woven Tile (page 22)
Use the chart for no. 46 (Woven Tile) for this design.

45 Fancy Chequerboard (page 22)
I wanted a design that had the same impact one gets from holding balls of yarn together instead of the fracturing that Fair Isle often creates. These large, brash shapes are good vehicles for bold use of saturated colour. Many close shades of two colours work best.

Chart note: Make the two corner-colours different at every meeting point.

46 Woven Tile (page 22)
Bathroom floor tiles in a Cincinnati hotel jumped to my attention and this design was born.

Chart note: Use a single colour for the rectangles and a single colour for the outlines throughout, working these two colours in the stranding technique. Use a different colour for each of the little squares and work them in intarsia (see pages 156 and 157).

47 Little Boxes (page 22)
This is one of my early designs and it still delights me. It's a delicious framework for colour and is easy to memorize once you get going.

Chart note: This is a section of the original chart for this design (see page 158). Keep changing the types of squares and the colours, and make up your own graphic combinations.

48 Birdbox

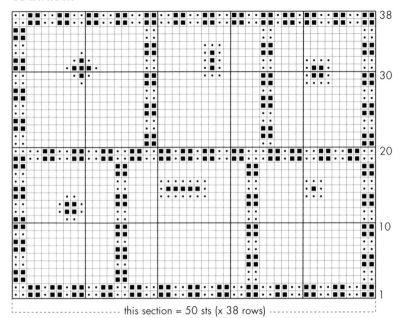

this section = 50 sts (x 38 rows)

49 Box Star Square

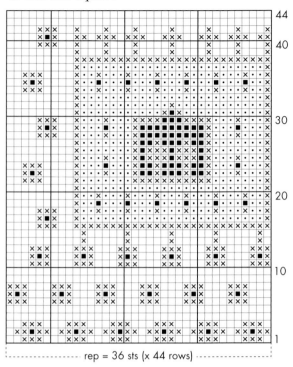

rep = 36 sts (x 44 rows)

50 Postage Stamp CHART 1

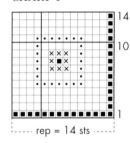

rep = 14 sts

50 Postage Stamp CHART 2

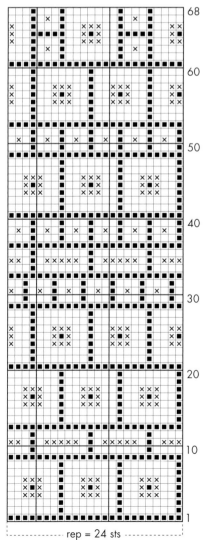

rep = 24 sts

50 Postage Stamp CHART 3

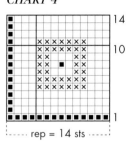

rep = 20 sts

50 Postage Stamp CHART 4

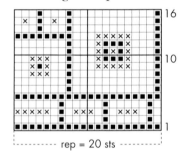

rep = 14 sts

50 Postage Stamp CHART 5

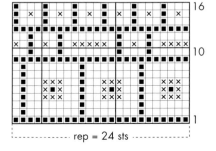

rep = 24 sts

48 Birdbox (page 22)
An old Oriental carpet I saw had this striking geometric design that translates so well into knitting. Don't the motifs look like birdboxes?
Chart note: This is only a section of the original chart where every square is a slightly different size and shape, but the scheme is easy to expand. Make the design bigger widthways by simply knitting more squares across the row and lengthways by continuing upwards with squares of different depths.

49 Box Star Square (page 23)
Chart note: Work the centre of the boxes in intarsia, so you don't have to carry the yarn across the entire row.

50 Postage Stamp (page 23)
I love stamps and this pattern, where the colours change only at the square centres, feels like a collection of similar stamps. Try different neutral background colours to see how they spark off the colour changes.
Chart note: Not all the motifs in this pattern have the same stitch-repeat, so it is divided into five charts. Use the charts on their own, or combine them, starting with Chart 1 then working Charts 2–5 in that order.

52 Letterboxes

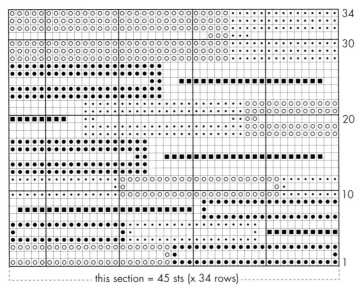

this section = 45 sts (x 34 rows)

51 Basket Squares

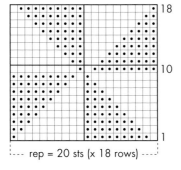

rep = 12 sts
(x 12 rows)

53 Chatterbox

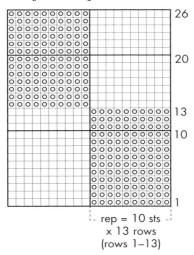

rep = 20 sts (x 18 rows)

54 African Squares

rep = 10 sts
x 13 rows
(rows 1–13)

55 Slabs

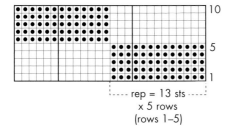

rep = 13 sts
x 5 rows
(rows 1–5)

56 Multicoloured Squares

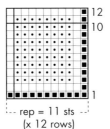

rep = 11 sts
(x 12 rows)

51 Basket Squares (page 23)
An Indonesian basket I have instigated this pattern. It was first used as a machine knit for the Penny Plain Company.
Chart note: This simple design uses only two colours a row and the two colours are changed every six rows.

52 Letterboxes (page 23)
To date I've never actually made anything in this design, so maybe you will beat me to it. The squashed scale of it is compelling and would look lovely on a cushion cover or waistcoat/vest.
Chart note: This is just a section of the design on the sample swatch it was taken from. Once you understand the random shapes (thin rectangles of different depths and widths with centre 'slots'), you can easily expand the design and work it directly onto your knitting without having to follow a chart.

53 Chatterbox (page 24)
Patchwork quilt motifs so often find their way into my knits – here is a classic.
Chart note: Use a different set of two colours for each 20-stitch by 18-row square.

54 African Squares (page 24)
Any close-tones palette would do for this simple but effective idea. Think of tiles, stone walls or army camouflage for your colour scheme.
Chart note: Instead of working the squares stacked exactly on top of each other as shown on the chart, to give the design more movement, you can work some or all of the individual rows of squares a stitch or two askew, so they are not stacked so precisely.

55 Slabs (page 24)
Brick-like slabs of colour are easy and motivating to knit, since you change colours just as you get bored with one set.

56 Multicoloured Squares
(page 25)
I made this as an extravagant one-off knit for an exhibition. The simple consistent square shows off the complexity of tone in the boxes.
Chart note: Change colours with each square, using different textures of yarns if desired.

57 Shirt Stripes (page 26)

Classic shirt stripes are always showstopping when combined. Bolts of fabric in tailor's shops get me going – this design does the same.

Chart note: The chart depicts only a section of the knitting. For a bigger design, use this as a starting point for your own chart. Draw randomly sized overlapping patches on the graph paper. As you knit, work a different stripe pattern into each patch shape, following your chart for the patch shape only.

58 Ribbon Design (page 27)

My enthusiasm for Victorian ribbon weave fabrics is reflected in this swatch. It suits many different colour schemes.

Chart note: The chart gives only a section of the original (see page 158) – it is enough to get you started. You can expand the design yourself by varying the width of the vertical 'ribbons' as you work across your knitting, and by varying the width of the horizontal 'ribbons' as you work upwards. Alternatively, you can use the chart as a stitch and row repeat.

59 Marble Blocks (page 27)

This featured in my book Glorious Inspirations. *It's taken from an ancient Venetian marble mosaic.*

Chart note: Use the tones suggested by the chart symbols or knitted sample to achieve a three-dimensional effect.

60 Mini-Roman Blocks No. 2 (page 27)

A fragment of Roman mosaic sent me flying to my knitting needles to work out this enticing geometric form. It makes a spirited patchwork quilt as well. See Green Granite Blocks *(design no. 66 on page 28) for a scaled-up version.*

Chart note: Use the tones suggested by the chart symbols or knitted sample to achieve a three-dimensional effect.

57 Shirt Stripes

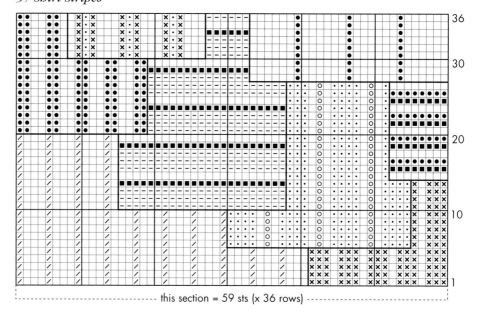

------- this section = 59 sts (x 36 rows) -------

58 Ribbon Design

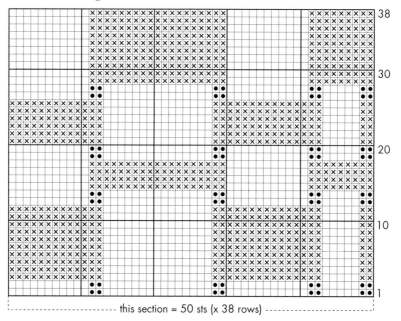

------- this section = 50 sts (x 38 rows) -------

59 Marble Blocks

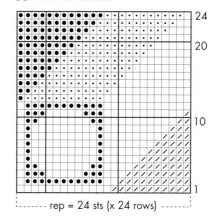

------ rep = 24 sts (x 24 rows) ------

60 Mini Roman Blocks No. 2

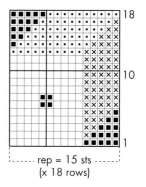

------ rep = 15 sts ------
(x 18 rows)

61 Jumbled Squares

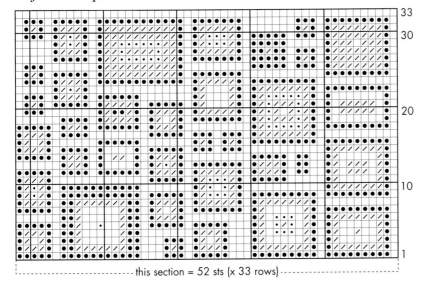

------------- this section = 52 sts (x 33 rows) -------------

61 Jumbled Squares (page 27)

Although this looks impressive and a killer to knit, it's quite easy with its dead straight angles. Have a go at your own version.

Chart note: The chart gives only a section of the original design, but you can use it as a repeat. Or, use it for the right-hand side of the design and reverse the design for the left side to create a mirror image, with the small squares at the left-hand side of the chart as the centre squares (see sample on page 27).

62 Ivory Squares (page 27)

A huge shawl in this pattern is shown in my book Glorious Knitting – *all tones of ivory, with delicate colour highlights. Try a long coat in these random squares.*

Chart note: The chart gives only a section of the design. If you want to make a bigger piece of knitting, expand the chart, overlapping random-size squares as shown here. Use different pale tones in each square.

62 Ivory Squares

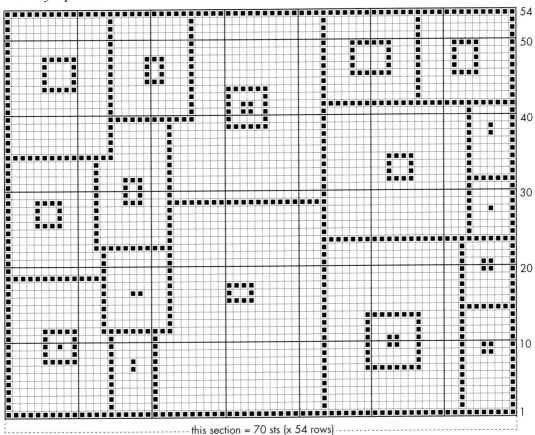

------------- this section = 70 sts (x 54 rows) -------------

63 Mitred Squares

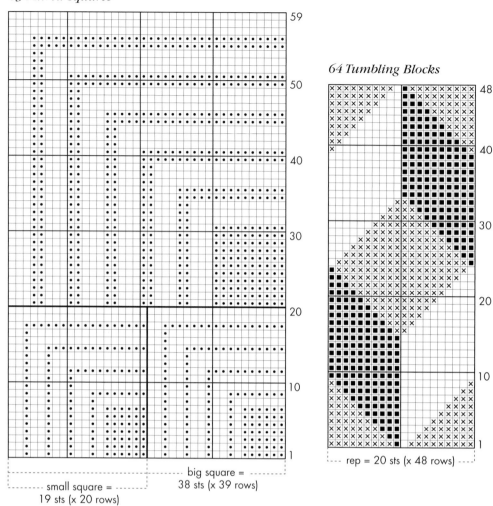

big square = 38 sts (x 39 rows)

small square = 19 sts (x 20 rows)

64 Tumbling Blocks

rep = 20 sts (x 48 rows)

65 Mini Roman Blocks No. 1

rep = 15 sts (x 84 rows)

66 Green Granite Blocks

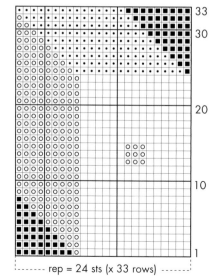

rep = 24 sts (x 33 rows)

63 Mitred Squares (page 27)

This bold design has been used in patchwork and as tiles. The knitter Horst Schultz has also featured it in many engaging patterns. It would make a mesmerizing cushion or waistcoat/vest design, or a smart boxy jacket.

Chart note: Use a different set of two colours for each square. Mix the two square sizes as desired.

64 Tumbling Blocks (page 28)

Decorative objects from tiles to patchwork carry this classic pattern. I first saw it knitted by designer Sasha Kagan in the 70's. The chart is very easy to memorize. Choose a colour palette that is bold, or close toned like marquetry woodwork.

Chart note: For a three-dimensional effect, use the tones suggested by the chart symbols or knitted sample.

65 Mini-Roman Blocks No. 1 (page 28)

Chart note: For a three-dimensional effect, use the tones suggested by the chart symbols or knitted sample.

66 Green Granite Blocks (page 28)

This scaled-up Mini-Roman Blocks (design no. 60 on page 94) looks good in neutral tones and works well when contrasting.

Chart note: For a three-dimensional effect, use the tones suggested by the chart symbols or knitted sample.

67 Floating Blocks (page 28)

I first saw this pleasing variation on Tumbling Blocks (design no. 64 on page 96) in an antique patchwork book.

Chart note: To create a three-dimensional effect, use the tones suggested by the chart symbols or knitted sample.

68 Shadow Boxes (page 29)

An old patchwork design called Attic Windows was the source for this format. It has a rhythmic, airy look.

Chart note: To create a three-dimensional effect, use the tones suggested by the chart symbols or knitted sample.

67 Floating Blocks

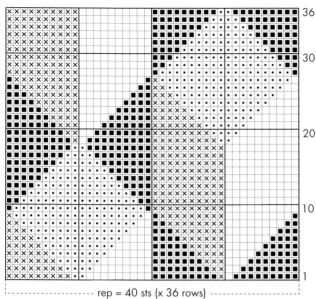

rep = 40 sts (x 36 rows)

68 Shadow Boxes

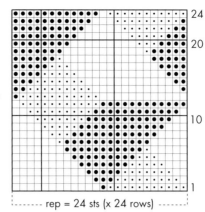

rep = 24 sts (x 24 rows)

69 Girder (page 29)

A floor design caught my eye for this knit. Although difficult to walk on, it makes a hell of a jacket pattern.

Chart note: Use the tones suggested by the chart symbols or knitted sample to achieve a three-dimensional effect.

70 Fan Box (page 29)

Another old patchwork block that really enthralls me. I've not found a use for it yet, but will one day.

Chart note: Use the tones suggested by the chart symbols or knitted sample to achieve a three-dimensional effect.

69 Girder

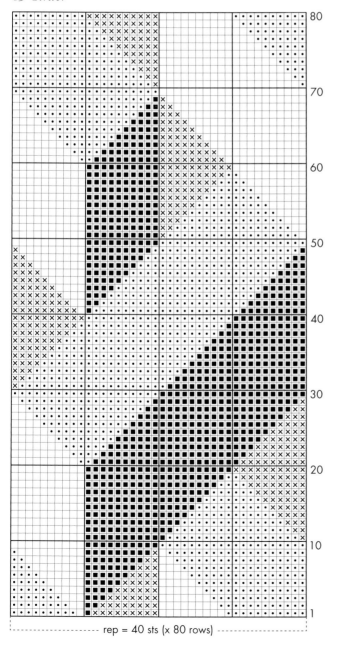

rep = 40 sts (x 80 rows)

70 Fan Box

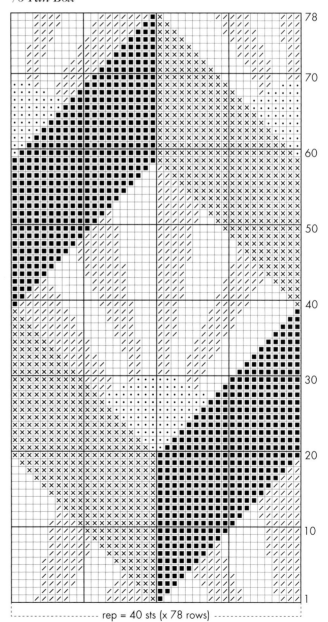

rep = 40 sts (x 78 rows)

71 Mosaic

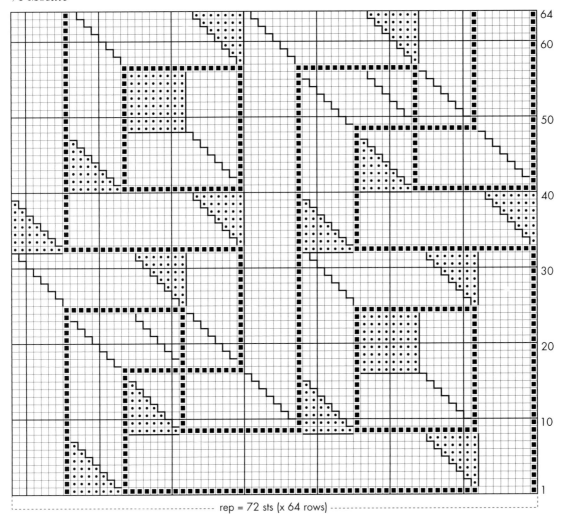

64
60
50
40
30
20
10
1

rep = 72 sts (x 64 rows)

72 Cross Patch

71 Mosaic (page 29)
A postcard with an old Ravenna mosaic came through the mail one day – this is the knitted rendition.
Chart note: For a three-dimensional effect, use the tones suggested by the chart symbols or knitted sample.

crosses

72 Cross Patch (page 30)
An alluring detail in a Gustav Klimpt painting led to this lively overlapping crosses pattern. There's no chart provided as it would be too big to include, but an advanced knitter could knit it up from the simple diagram with a little patience and lots of enthusiasm.

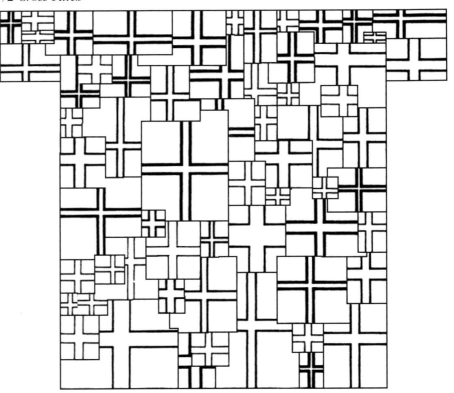

73 Small-Scale Cross Patch

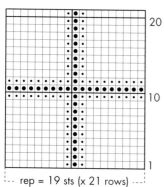

rep = 19 sts (x 21 rows)

75 Byzantine

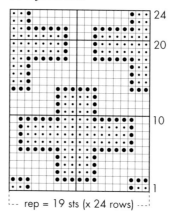

rep = 19 sts (x 24 rows)

74 Big Crosses

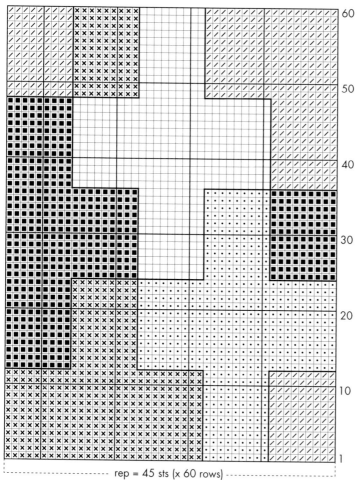

rep = 45 sts (x 60 rows)

73 Small-Scale Cross Patch
(page 31)
*A simplified version of the large
Cross Patch (see design no. 72
on page 30).*
Chart note: Use a different set
of colours for each 19-stitch by
21-row square.

74 Big Crosses (page 31)
*A much easier to knit version of
Icon (see design no. 77 on page
31), this is great on a really
large-scale coat or full jacket. It
would look excellent in black
and white.*
Chart note: Use a different
colour or set of toning colours
for each cross.

75 Byzantine (page 31)
*Here's a simple offshoot of Icon
(see design no. 77 on page 31).*
Chart note: Keep the cross
outlines in similar hues, but fill
in each cross with a different
colour. Work the background in
subtly toning shades.

76 Lumberjack (page 31)
*An old fabric print of a plaid,
which had roughly this layout,
caught my eye. It knitted up
quite easily, so here it is. The
pattern makes me think of
Canadian work jackets.*
Chart note: Work the blank
squares on the chart (the
background) in toning shades,
carrying the yarn across each
row. Work the 'four-paned
windows' in different colours,
using the intarsia technique.

76 Lumberjack

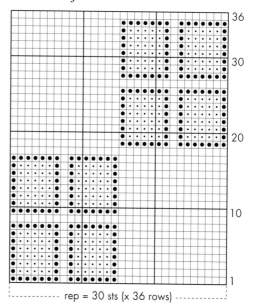

rep = 30 sts (x 36 rows)

77 *Icon*

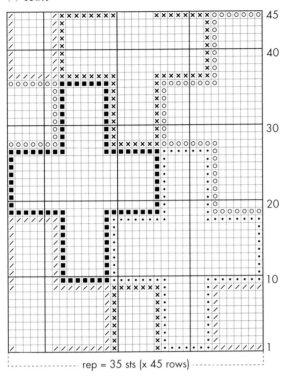

rep = 35 sts (x 45 rows)

78 *Chequerboard*

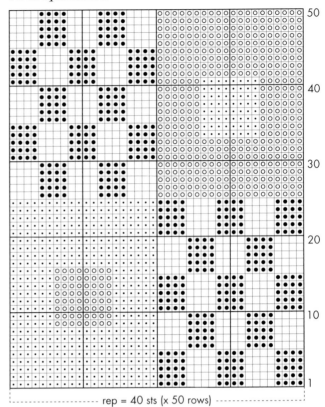

rep = 40 sts (x 50 rows)

77 Icon (page 31)

This classic overlapping cross pattern was born out of my love of Russian icons. On the icons, the crosses are usually black and white, but my weakness is lashings of colour whenever possible.

Chart note: Use a different outline colour and filling-in colour for each cross.

patches

78 Chequerboard (page 32)

The idea for this easy but atmospheric knit came from an old carpet. I've also done a patchwork of it.

79 Contrast Stripe Patch
(page 32)

I find stripes on stripes stunning and this large-scale design shows that well. Try it for a big coat, curtains or a bedcover.

Chart note: The chart shows only a section of the knit design, but you can easily make your own chart on graph paper to expand the design. Just draw overlapping patch outlines like these and fill them in with stripes as you knit.

79 *Contrast Stripe Patch*

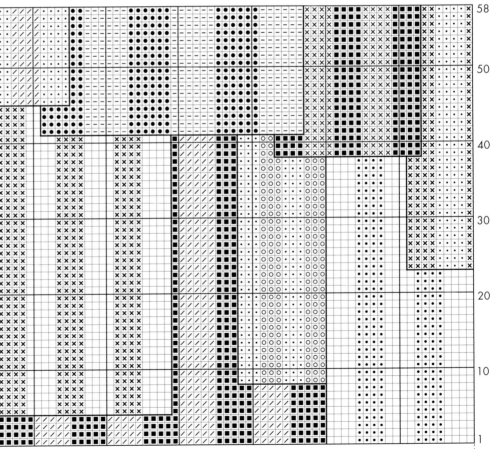

this section = 65 sts (x 58 rows)

80 Small Steps CHART 1

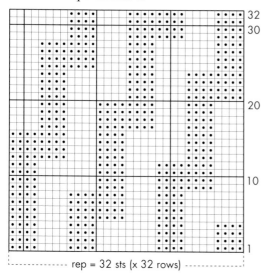

rep = 32 sts (x 32 rows)

80 Small Steps CHART 2

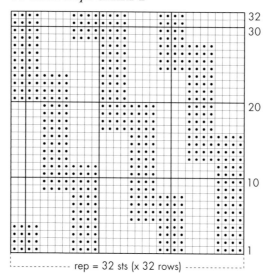

rep = 32 sts (x 32 rows)

81 Medium Steps

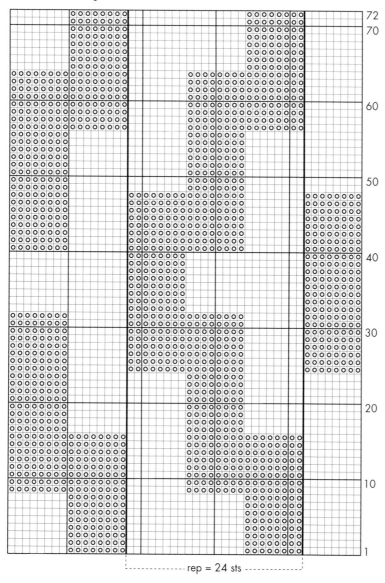

rep = 24 sts

80 Small Steps (page 32)
Stonework, baskets and tiles often feature this basic step pattern. It knits up easily and strikingly.
Chart note: Use one or other of the charts on its own, or combine them on the same piece of knitting by working one side in each diagonal.

81 Medium Steps (page 32)
Chart note: The full chart is too big to include here, so only a section of it is given. Once you get going you can work it without a chart. Work the 8-stitch wide stripes to the height desired, then make a 'step' to the left as shown. Work upwards in this way until you want to begin making steps up to the right.

82 Red Patch (page 33)
Stone walls, overlapping carpet laid out to dry and tiles on a roof make fabulous patterns. Here's an interpretation of that type of layout.

Chart note: The chart gives only a section of this design (see page 158). Make a bigger chart yourself if you need a larger piece of knitting. Knit each patch a different colour.

83 Overlapping Patch (page 33)
This is surprisingly easy to knit as each patch starts whole and is interrupted by subsequent patches overlapping it. Have a go at your own version if you need a bigger chart.

82 Red Patch

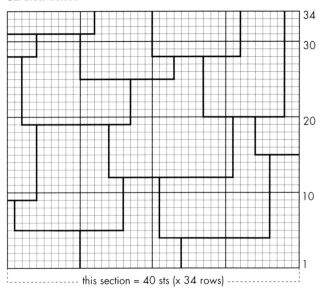

----------- this section = 40 sts (x 34 rows) -----------

83 Overlapping Patch

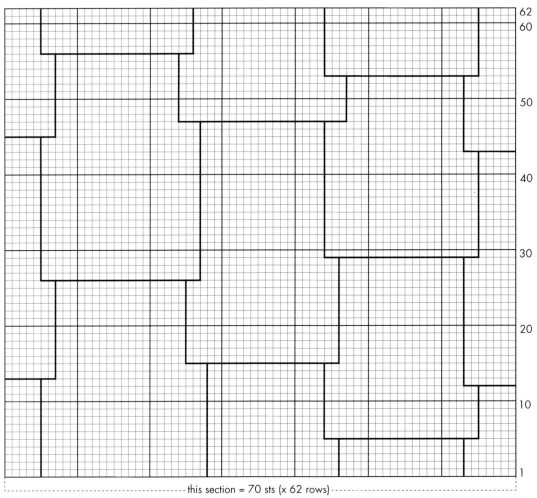

----------- this section = 70 sts (x 62 rows) -----------

84 Dot Patch

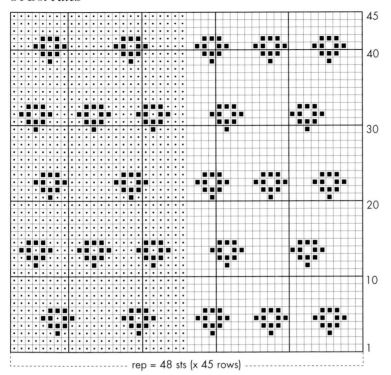

45
40
30
20
10
1

-------- rep = 48 sts (x 45 rows) --------

84 Dot Patch (page 33)
Another design I've done for the Peruvian Connection mail-order catalogue, this one based on an old Indian weave.
Chart note: Use different toning shades for each box and work them in the intarsia technique. Carry the yarn for the little motifs across the back of the work.

85 Watermelon Stripe (page 33)
Chart note: The chart gives only a section of the design, but you can easily expand it by drawing patch outlines on your graph paper and knitting stripes inside each patch as you proceed.

85 Watermelon Stripe

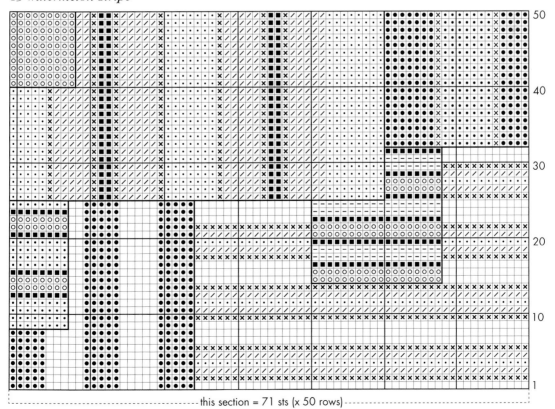

50
40
30
20
10
1

-------- this section = 71 sts (x 50 rows) --------

87 Moody Blues

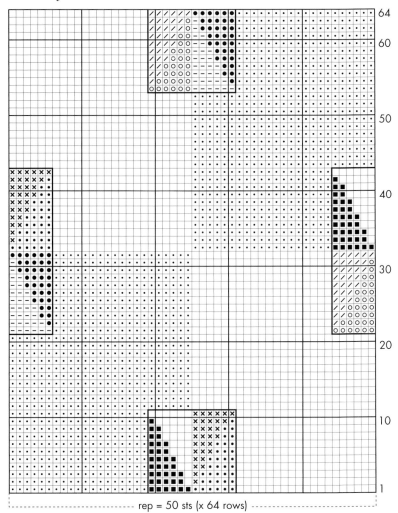

rep = 50 sts (x 64 rows)

86 Cones

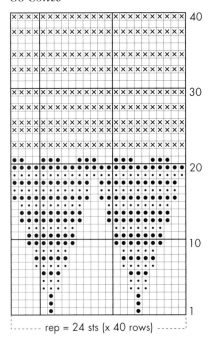

rep = 24 sts (x 40 rows)

triangles

86 Cones (page 34)

English roadworks are studded with orange cones, so we see a lot of them. I tried to make this annoying sight into something attractive. This is a good knit for beginners.

Chart note: The symbols on the chart show where to position stripe changes, but introduce as many stripe colours as desired. This is a simple one- and two-colours-a-row design.

87 Moody Blues (page 34)

Chart note: See sample swatch on page 34 for colour ideas.

88 Patchwork Triangles (page 34)

The basis for this design is a patchwork pattern called Lady of the Lake. It's very effective in many colour schemes – I can't wait to see what you come up with.

Chart note: Work each large split diamond in a different set of two colours. Work the small triangles in the same two contrasting colours.

88 Patchwork Triangles

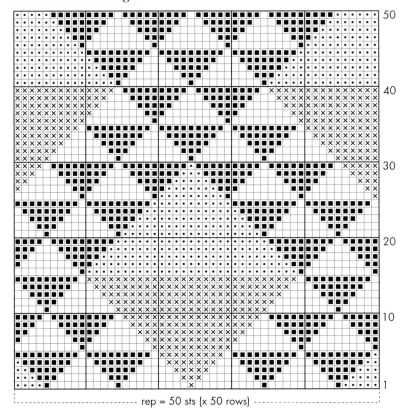

rep = 50 sts (x 50 rows)

89 Toothed Stripe

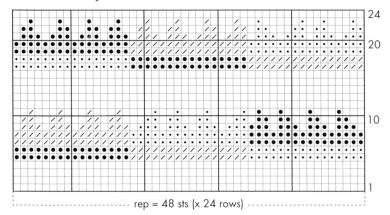

rep = 48 sts (x 24 rows)

90 Stepped Triangles

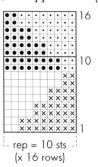

rep = 10 sts
(x 16 rows)

91 Pennants

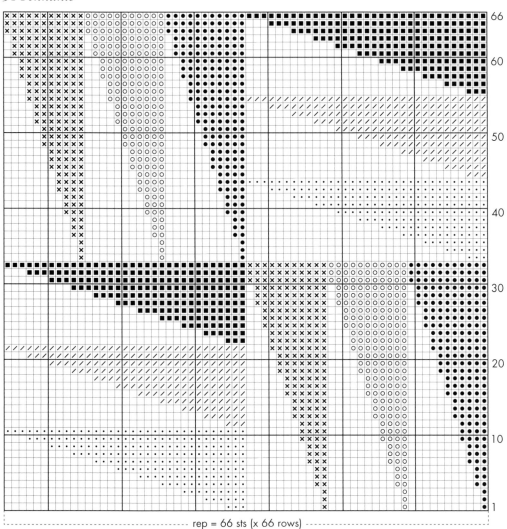

rep = 66 sts (x 66 rows)

89 Toothed Stripe (page 34)
Probably one of my most popular designs, this spiky stripe makes a great border and it begs to be interpreted in many different colour combos. I found a similar pattern as a detail on a painted boat.
Chart note: Change colours for tooth motifs as suggested by the symbols and work stripes in the background (blank squares).

90 Stepped Triangles (page 34)
An ethnic basket sparked off the idea for this design. It works well on a tiny or large scale.
Chart note: Use a different set of two colours for every 10-row-high row of triangles.

91 Pennants (page 35)
A furnishing fabric was the source for the basic outlines for this design. I've also used this layout for a large patchwork – a knitted version would make just as impressive a blanket.
Chart note: Change colours in each square of triangles and work some triangles in stripes of toning shades.

92 Banded Triangle (page 36)

A book on old Japanese brocades was the source for these Banded Triangles. I love the sharp graphic nature of the design. It's very flattering as a jacket motif.

Chart note: Change the outline and triangle colour for each large triangle.

93 Super Triangle (page 36)

My first big success with a Rowan Yarns kit, this was featured in the Woman and Home *magazine in Britain. It got thousands of people knitting with colour for the first time. There are only two colours to deal with in each row.*

Chart note: Combine the various triangle sizes at random up your knitting by working the full row-repeat of a chart before moving on to the next chart.

92 Banded Triangle

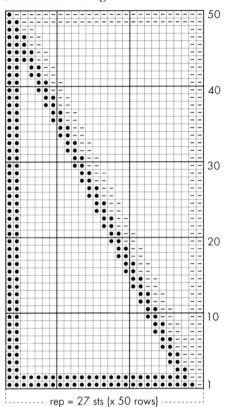

rep = 27 sts (x 50 rows)

93 Super Triangle
CHART 1

rep = 6 sts (x 5 rows)

93 Super Triangle
CHART 2

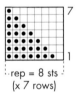

rep = 8 sts (x 7 rows)

93 Super Triangle
CHART 3

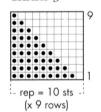

rep = 10 sts (x 9 rows)

93 Super Triangle
CHART 4

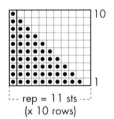

rep = 11 sts (x 10 rows)

93 Super Triangle
CHART 5

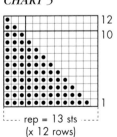

rep = 13 sts (x 12 rows)

93 Super Triangle
CHART 6

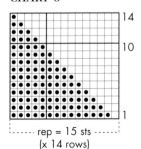

rep = 15 sts (x 14 rows)

93 Super Triangle
CHART 7

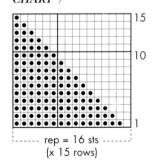

rep = 16 sts (x 15 rows)

94 Feathers

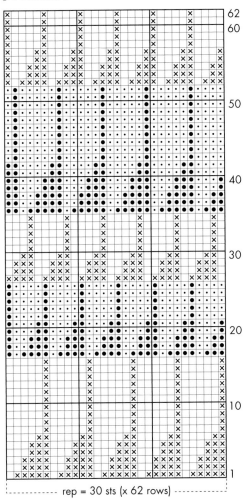

rep = 30 sts (x 62 rows)

95 Facets

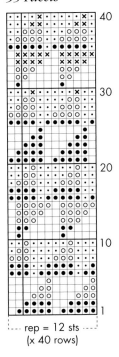

rep = 12 sts
(x 40 rows)

97 Japanese Triangles

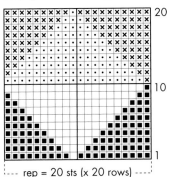

rep = 20 sts (x 20 rows)

94 Feathers (page 36)
This feather design has a nice long look, so it makes a good slimming coat.
Chart note: Change sets of colours for each horizontal row of feathers.

95 Facets (page 36)
An intricate finely pieced patchwork called Broken Dishes inspired this design. It's quick and easy to knit.
Chart note: This pattern has only two colours in each row. Every other triangle across a line of triangles is solid, and every other triangle is worked in random stripes. The triangles will point upwards or downwards depending on the tone of colours you use. Once you get going you don't have to follow the chart exactly.

96 Pinwheel (page 36)
With its impressive bold outline, this patchwork classic makes such a good knit that I've done it in many different scales and colour palettes. It's a perfect vehicle for playing with contrast and close tone schemes.
Chart note: Use a different set of colours for each big square.

97 Japanese Triangles (page 37)
Yet another strong, simple geometric inspired by the ever-resourceful Japanese artists.
Chart note: Change colours with each triangle and work occasional triangles in three stripes.

96 Pinwheel

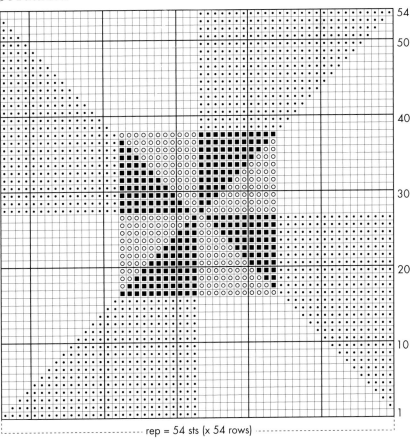

rep = 54 sts (x 54 rows)

98 Big Diamond

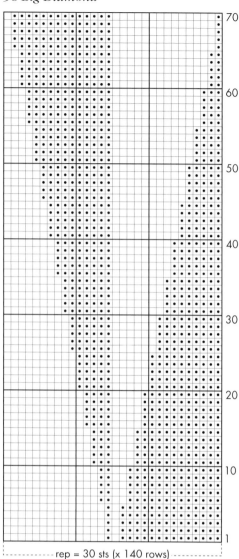

rep = 30 sts (x 140 rows)

99 Weave Variation

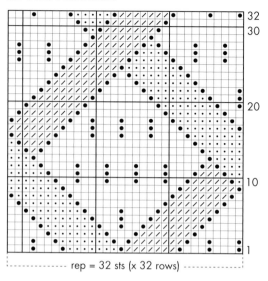

rep = 32 sts (x 32 rows)

100 Puzzle

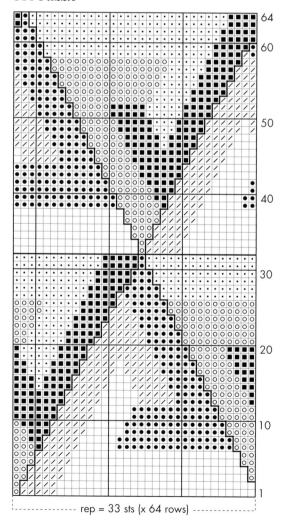

rep = 33 sts (x 64 rows)

diamonds

98 Big Diamond (page 38)

Give these wonderful audacious diamonds as much colour shading as you can throughout – the design will still provide a slim line for any body shape. The big gals love this one.

Chart note: Work each triangle in gradually blending shades. The full row repeat is 140 rows long – after chart row 70, turn the chart upside down and read it back to chart row 1.

99 Weave Variation (page 38)

Chart note: Use different colours for the diagonal stripes and toning colours in the diamonds.

100 Puzzle (page 39)

I designed Puzzle, an Islamic format, in stranded pima cotton for the Peruvian Connection mail-order catalogue. The intricate geometry is charming in close tweedy tones, but it could be knit in highly contrasting colours for a vigorous graphic effect.

101 Shaded Diamond (page 39)

Here's a simple layout given delicious movement by simple shading.

Chart note: Use a different set of closely toned shades in each diamond.

101 Shaded Diamond

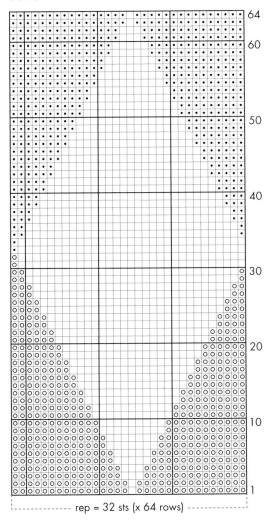

rep = 32 sts (x 64 rows)

102 Lattice

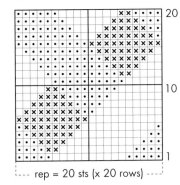

rep = 20 sts (x 20 rows)

103 Chinese Basket

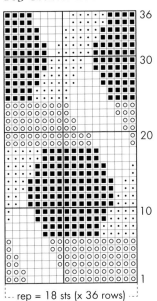

rep = 18 sts (x 36 rows)

102 Lattice (page 39)
Chart note: Use a different colour for each diagonal stripe and very dark colours for the diamonds between the diagonals.

103 Chinese Basket (page 39)
This wide, open basket weave can be airy and light in soft colours, or dark and elegant. Its crisp lines are enticing.

104 Shaded Diamond (page 39)
Use the chart for no. 101 (Shaded Diamond) for this design.

105 Tile Lattice (page 40)
Another good design from a splendid tile floor layout.
Chart note: Use the same colour scheme throughout for the diagonal lattice and a different colour for each of the small diamonds at the lattice crossings. Fill in each large diamond with a different set of toning stripes.

106 Venetian Diamond (page 40)
A marble mosaic in Venice led to this knit. It is very exciting and graphic if worked in chunky yarn, for a jacket say.
Chart note: Work all the diamonds in the same three colours, or work each diamond in a different set of three colours.

105 Tile Lattice

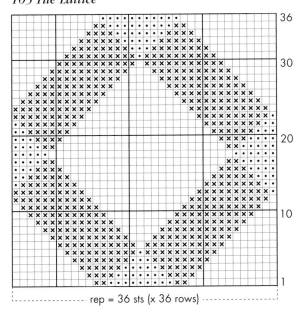

rep = 36 sts (x 36 rows)

106 Venetian Diamond

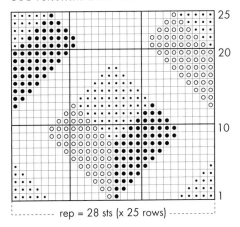

rep = 28 sts (x 25 rows)

107 Overlapping Diamonds
(page 40)

This is the sort of idea that you will find easier to just wing, and to do your own version of without a knitting chart. It's great fun to see how many colours you can use in it.

Chart note: The chart gives only a section of the original design. If you need a bigger chart, make one of your own or try creating new diamonds as you knit.

108 Tile Diamonds (page 41)

Chart note: Try this as a two-colours-a-row design.

109 Brick Diamond (page 41)

The close neutral tones of this knit were taken from typical yellow house bricks in London.

Chart note: Work each diamond in a different set of toning stripes.

110 Stepped Diamond
(page 41)

Chart note: Work each diamond in stripes of toning shades.

107 Overlapping Diamonds

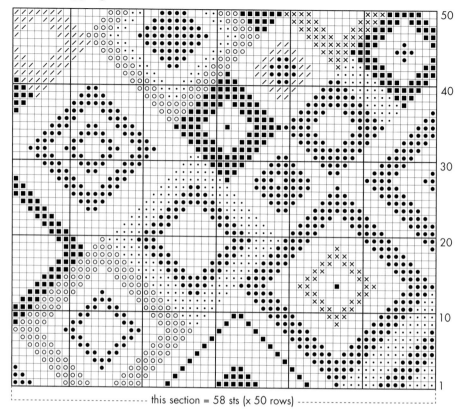

this section = 58 sts (x 50 rows)

108 Tile Diamonds

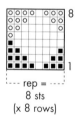

rep =
8 sts
(x 8 rows)

110 Stepped Diamond

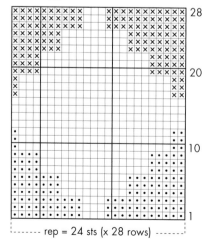

rep = 24 sts (x 28 rows)

109 Brick Diamond

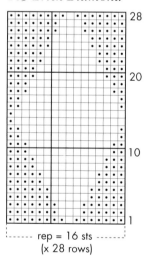

rep = 16 sts
(x 28 rows)

111 Blue Diamonds

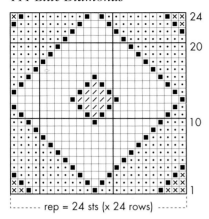

rep = 24 sts (x 24 rows)

113 Guatemala Diamonds

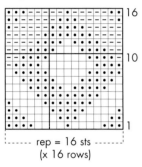

rep = 16 sts
(x 16 rows)

115 Courthouse Steps

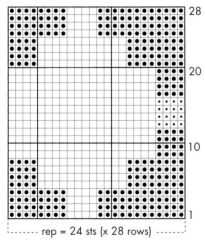

rep = 24 sts (x 28 rows)

112 Red Diamonds

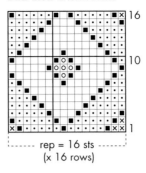

rep = 16 sts
(x 16 rows)

114 Split Diamond

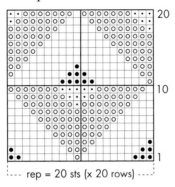

rep = 20 sts (x 20 rows)

116 Midnight Harlequin

rep =
8 sts
(x 12 rows)

117 Outlined Star

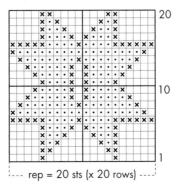

rep = 20 sts (x 20 rows)

111 Blue Diamonds (page 42)
A book on Indian embroidery had a piece with an intense all-over pattern that gave birth to the idea for my Blue and Red Diamonds knits. Just take any colour that you love and use as many close shades of it as you can, adding in those delicious kick colours.
Chart note: See sample on page 42 for colour ideas.

112 Red Diamonds (page 42)
See comments and Chart note for Blue Diamonds (design no. 111).

113 Guatemala Diamonds (page 42)
This design was often used in ancient South American textiles. It's an easy pattern to knit since it has such a logical progression (like Tumbling Blocks, design no. 64 on page 28). The blast of contrasting colours was inspired by a country with one of the most colourful cultures on the planet.
Chart note: Use different colours for each diamond.

114 Split Diamond (page 43)
Chart note: See sample on page 43 for colour ideas.

115 Courthouse Steps (page 43)
My book Passionate Patchwork *features this same pattern. I couldn't resist seeing how it would look in knitting.*
Chart note: To unify the design, use the same colour throughout for the little squares. Use a different colour or set of toning colours for each diamond.

116 Midnight Harlequin (page 43)
Things taken to extremes fascinate me and this dark diamond is a case in point. You could make this all pearl tones or deep reds or any other colours you are drawn to.
Chart note: Use a single colour for the background (black was used here) and carry it across each row. Choose a different colour for each diamond and work them in intarsia.

stars

117 Outlined Star (page 44)
My passion for old carpets has led to many of my designs and this is one of them. It was the first star I knitted and looked dazzling on large floor-length coats and short jackets. The outline makes it very crisp.

111

118 Summer Star (page 44)
This star pattern comes directly from the patchwork world where it is often stitched in patterned cloth.

119 Circus Star (page 44)
A fresh, dead easy knit, this is great for kids' sweaters in any colours you can dream up.

120 Bold Star (page 44)
This is a large-scale version of Outlined Star (see design no. 117 on page 44).

121 Desert Stars (page 45)
I don't remember where I found this shape of star, but I used it for the centre of a large knitted blanket commissioned for a New York apartment.

Chart note: The chart gives only a section of the original blanket design, where all the star shapes are similar but not exactly the same (see page 155). You can use the chart rows 12–66 as a repeat or make your own large chart with slightly different stars all over it.

118 Summer Star

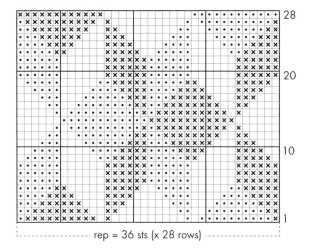

rep = 36 sts (x 28 rows)

119 Circus Star

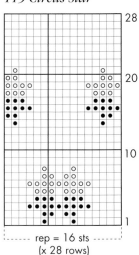

rep = 16 sts
(x 28 rows)

121 Desert Stars

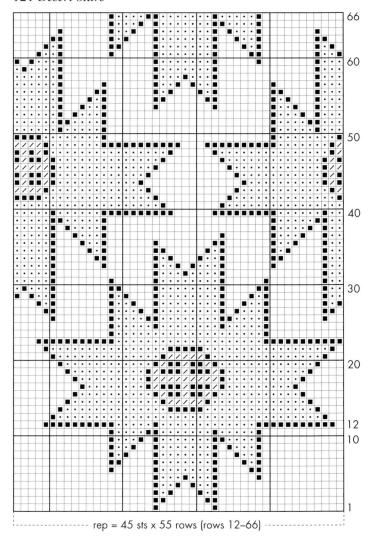

rep = 45 sts x 55 rows (rows 12–66)

120 Bold Star

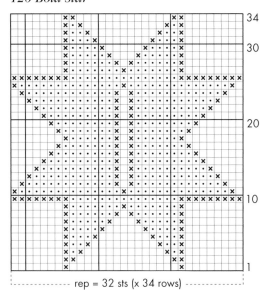

rep = 32 sts (x 34 rows)

122 Whirling Star

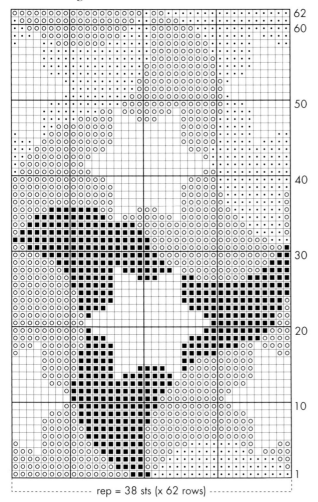

rep = 38 sts (x 62 rows)

122 Whirling Star (page 46)

An Islamic configuration, this pattern is found in similar form on old tile walls in places like the Alhambra in Spain. The world of Islamic decoration is full of geometric beauty, and this compelling star is a shining example.

Chart note: Use a different set of colours for each star and surrounding whirl.

123 Box Star (page 46)

This adaptation of a sharp little star on a carpet was designed for a small jacket for the Peruvian Connection mail-order catalogue.

Chart note: Use the intarsia method to knit this design (see page 157).

124 Triangle Star (page 46)

Chart note: See sample on page 46 for colour ideas.

124 Triangle Star

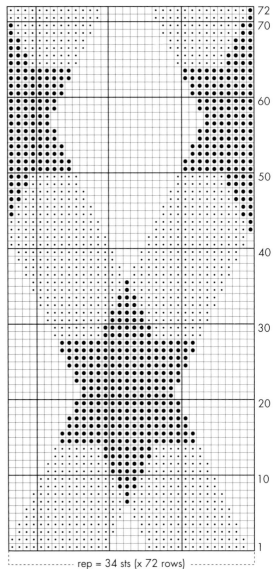

rep = 34 sts (x 72 rows)

123 Box Star

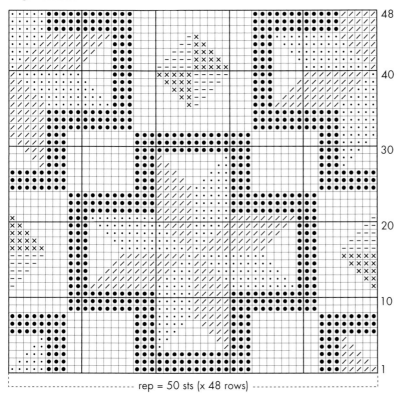

rep = 50 sts (x 48 rows)

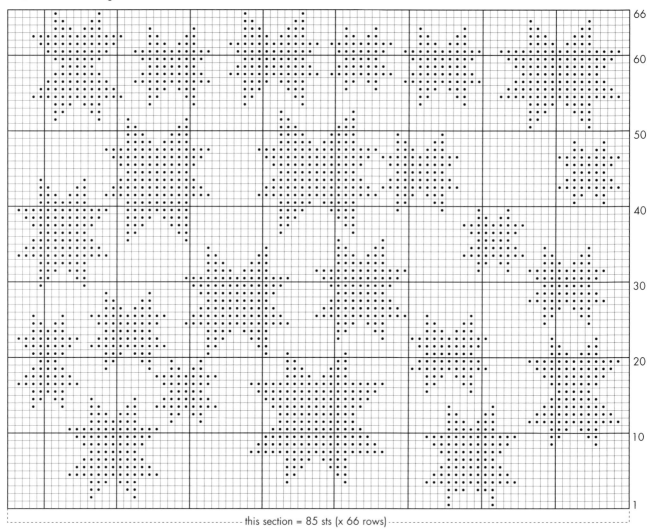

---- this section = 85 sts (x 66 rows) ----

126 Lone Star

125 Stars and Stripes (page 46)
Stars and Stripes would make a fantastic cushion cover, or a charming baby blanket with several borders around the stars.
Chart note: If you wish, work concentric stripes in the background (7 stitches wide and 7 rows deep). For a bigger piece of knitting, just add more random stars.

126 Lone Star (page 47)
This is one of my favourite new star ideas. The movement created by the shading is almost eerie.
Chart note: Work the stars in toning shades, starting with darker colours at the bottom and getting lighter towards the top tip. The background on the sample is black (big dots on chart) with three rows of charcoal (small dots on chart).

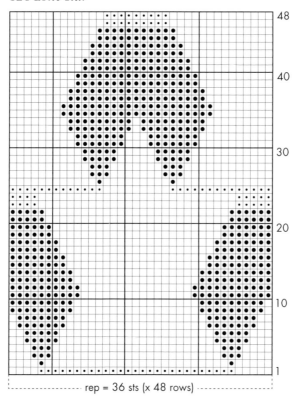

---- rep = 36 sts (x 48 rows) ----

114

127 Geometric Star

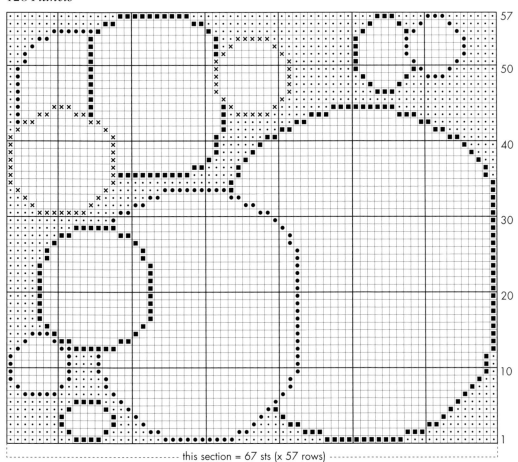

- - - - rep = 54 sts (x 34 rows) - - - -

127 Geometric Star (page 47)

Deliciously complex, Geometric Star looks like one of my toughest designs to knit. But when you get started, you'll find each section is only two colours a row, so it is surprisingly manageable. Try a startlingly different colourway.

Chart note: The original chart for a jacket has a wider variety of patterns in the hexagons (see page 158). Make up your own simple two-colour patterns for them if you like.

circles

128 Planets (page 48)

I feel very proud of this design as I made it up entirely on the needles; no graph paper was used. While improvising, the changes in scale and tone seemed to develop quite naturally! Try winging your own version of circles.

Chart note: The chart gives only a section of the full design. For a bigger piece of knitting, and if you feel making it up on the needles is too difficult, make your own large chart with randomly sized overlapping circles like these. Draw them a little taller than wide as they become shorter on the knitted fabric.

128 Planets

- - - - this section = 67 sts (x 57 rows) - - - -

129 Peacock Spots (page 49)

Chart note: The chart shows a simple repeat of the irregular circle shapes in the design. After working the first two rows of circles, continue the row-repeat (rows 11–40) without the 'stems' (see swatch on page 49). If desired, add energy to the design by making up your own circle shapes so no two circles look the same.

130 Domino (page 49)

Dot patterns have always delighted me. These dots on solid grounds remind me of jockey outfits. You could do it in sassy contrasting racing colours.

Chart note: Change the colour of the background (the blank squares) and dot colour with each square (which is 28 stitches wide and 26 rows tall).

131 Floating Circles (page 50)

When I was about to go on TV in Australia, I noticed a smart black box of eye shadows in circular pans – it was only a matter of time before it turned into this knit.

Chart note: Work each circle in different colours.

129 Peacock Spots

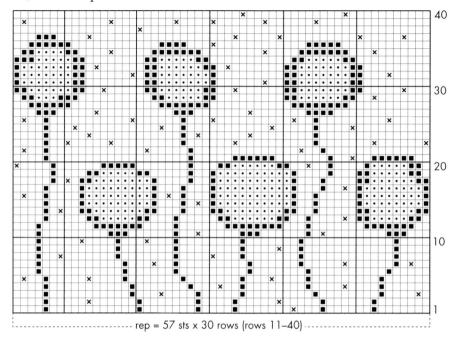

rep = 57 sts x 30 rows (rows 11–40)

130 Domino

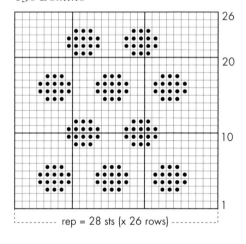

rep = 28 sts (x 26 rows)

131 Floating Circles

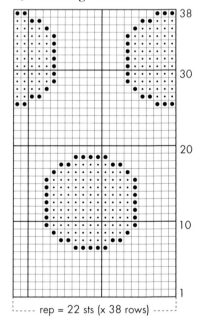

rep = 22 sts (x 38 rows)

132 Ping Pong

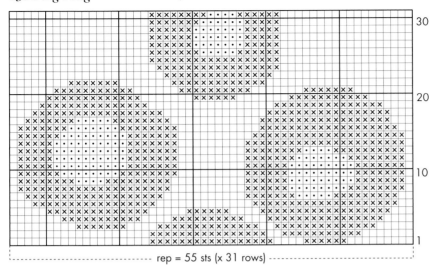

rep = 55 sts (x 31 rows)

133 Stone Circles

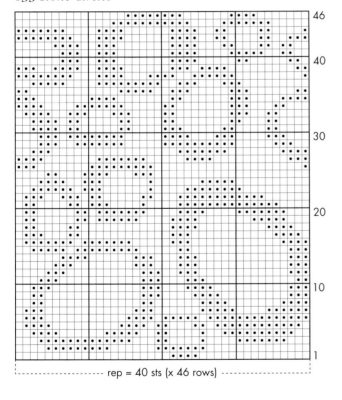

rep = 40 sts (x 46 rows)

134 Mini Floating Circles

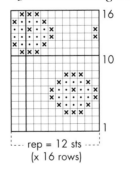

rep = 12 sts
(x 16 rows)

135 Persian Poppy

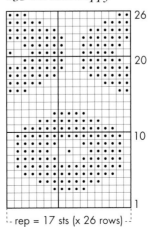

rep = 17 sts (x 26 rows)

132 Ping Pong (page 51)
Ping Pong was inspired by the great Austrian painter Gustav Klimpt. (See pages 6 and 7 for different colourways.)
Chart note: The chart gives only a section of the randomly shaped circles on the original, but it can be used as an all-over repeat. Use different colours for each circle.

133 Stone Circles (page 51)
A Tibetan pattern suggested this cool, grey study of miniature circles. People who are a bit nervous of my usual full-on colour enjoy this colour palette.
Chart note: The chart gives only a section of the original design (which is full of randomly shaped circles), but it can be used as an all-over repeat. Work the toning background stripes through the circle centres as well.

134 Mini Floating Circles (page 51)
Make this sharp, tight little pattern lively with a black ground, or delicate and soft with pastels. Try other looks, too.

135 Persian Poppy (page 52)
This is my 'Top of the Pops' – my greatest hit by far from my first knitting book Glorious Knitting. *I've seen this all over the world, in every colour scheme you can imagine. It looks good for anything from cushion covers to jackets. To work it with only two colours in a row, first make two balls of yarn. Tie together various lengths of about twenty colours for the background ball of yarn, and twenty close tones that contrast with the background for the poppy. Then just knit from the chart. (See pages 152 and 153 for different colourways.)*

136 Big Circle

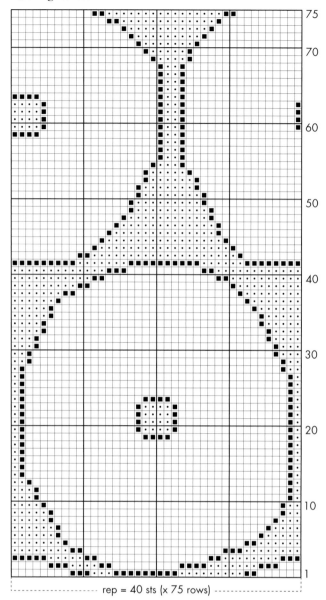

rep = 40 sts (x 75 rows)

137 Bead Lattice

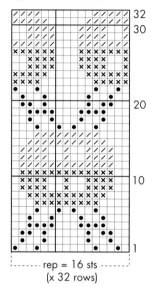

rep = 16 sts
(x 32 rows)

138 China Clouds

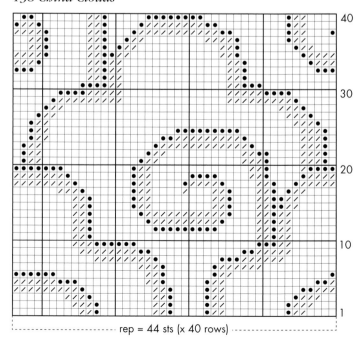

rep = 44 sts (x 40 rows)

136 Big Circle (pages 52-53)

The work of the Russian Ballet costume designer Bakst suggested this idea to me. He often used big powerful circles on his Oriental costumes. A great design for a long coat or stole. Use different textures of yarn for the full effect.

Chart note: Follow this chart repeat, or make your own chart and draw large, vaguely round circles on graph paper – they will give squashed circles when knit up.

137 Bead Lattice (page 54)

Can't you see this as a joyful child's sweater, or in an Oriental palette for cushions?

Chart note: Easy to knit, the Bead Lattice is worked with only two colours a row.

138 China Clouds (pages 54-55)

I love the old embroidered Chinese robes with coloured clouds above borders of stripes. This knit dramatizes those curling clouds.

Chart note: The original design has entirely irregular cloud shapes, but the chart gives a simple repeat. If you like, make your own big chart with similar irregular shapes.

118

139 Houses and Roses CHART 1

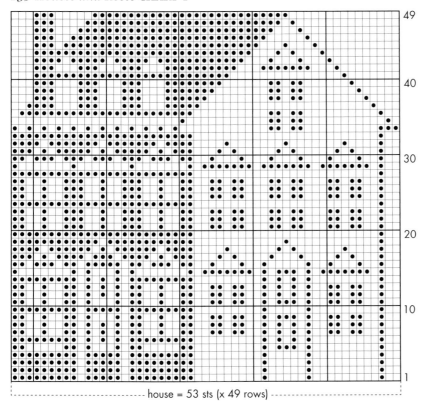

------ house = 53 sts (x 49 rows) ------

139 Houses and Roses CHART 3

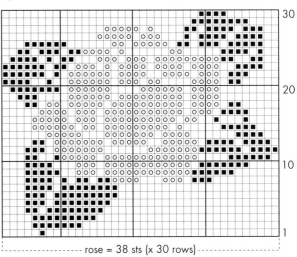

------ rose = 38 sts (x 30 rows) ------

houses

139 Houses and Roses (page 58)
This design echoes the graphic manner of houses on the early American coverlets. Being me, I added roses for a romantic twist! The houses could be arranged to strong masculine effect – without the rose, of course.

Chart note: Arrange the houses on your knitting however you like. Add the roses at random, so they overlap or underlap the houses.

139 Houses and Roses CHART 2

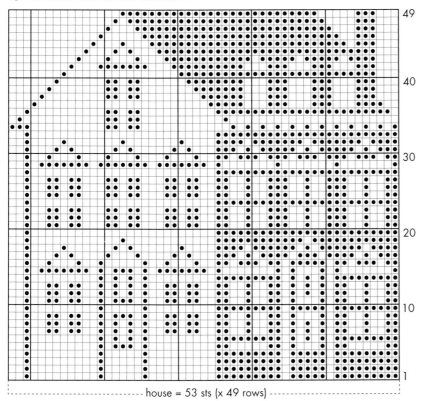

------ house = 53 sts (x 49 rows) ------

140 Tents (page 58)

This simple design appeared in one of my patchworks first, and then on a knit. It is a pattern that definitely changes when done on a massively different scale. Try it on a waistcoat in fine yarns, or on a blanket in chunky yarns.

Chart note: Use the chart repeat for your all-over pattern, or vary the number of vertical stripes across the tents, working four, five or seven stripes. You can also start with a row of tents that are 40-rows tall, then make each of the following rows of tents gradually shorter as you work upwards, making them 40, 30, then 20 rows tall under the rooftops.

141 Houses (page 58)

A hooked rag rug in the American museum in Bath put me on track for this popular knit. I've done it in tweedy colours, but it would look jaunty in solid colours.

Chart note: Place the houses one stitch and one row apart on your knitting. Use them as a border or an all-over design.

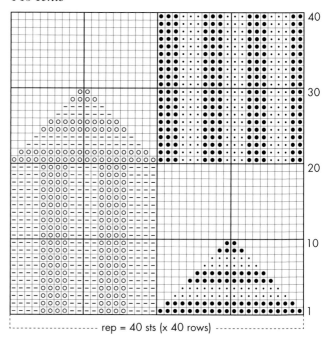

140 Tents

rep = 40 sts (x 40 rows)

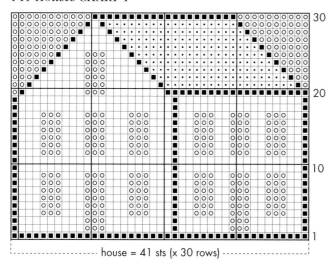

141 Houses CHART 1

house = 41 sts (x 30 rows)

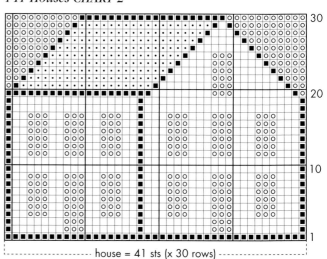

141 Houses CHART 2

house = 41 sts (x 30 rows)

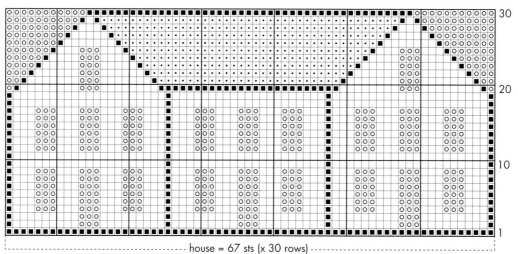

141 Houses CHART 3

house = 67 sts (x 30 rows)

142 Townhouses

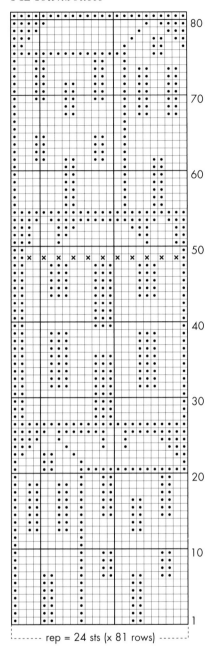

------ rep = 24 sts (x 81 rows) ------

143 Schoolhouses

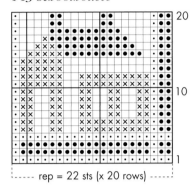

------ rep = 22 sts (x 20 rows) ------

142 Townhouses (page 58)
Townhouses was designed for the machine-knit company Penny Plain. It's an easy two-colours-a-row pattern.

143 Schoolhouses (page 58)
I spotted abstract houses like this on a patchwork and loved the effect of them row by row, separated by sashing borders.
Chart note: Keep the sashing borders and the rooftops the same colours throughout to unify the design, but use a different colour for each house and background.

144 Housetops (page 59)
Worked in many colours, this creates a busky all-over pattern. To make a good border, use toning shades or the same contrasting colours in every other row of housetops.

144 Housetops

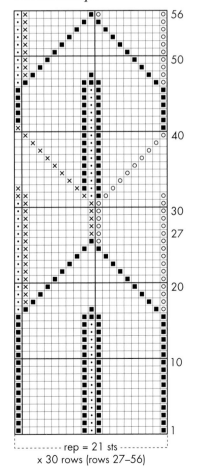

------- rep = 21 sts ---------
x 30 rows (rows 27–56)

145 Peruvian Cats

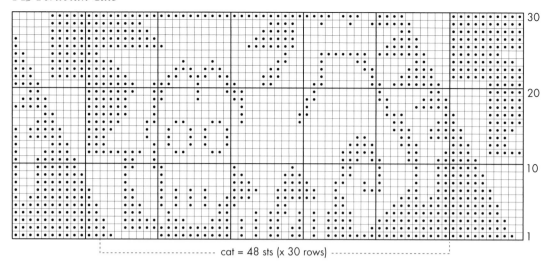

cat = 48 sts (x 30 rows)

146 Foolish Virgins

creatures

145 Peruvian Cats
(page 60)
Another old Peruvian-inspired knit for the Peruvian Connection catalogue. It is knit here in blue and cream, but it could be black and white or multicoloured as the fancy takes you.
Chart note: Use the cat motif singly or in a row in a border. To create an all-over diagonal cat pattern with diagonal steps between them, position the following cats as indicated at the edges of the chart.

146 Foolish Virgins
(page 60)
These magnificent figures come from an old Norwegian tapestry of the Bible story, 'The Foolish Virgins', hanging in a museum in Oslo. Try to maintain a little contrast in the colours, but experiment with your own schemes.
Chart note: The chart contains two of the four Foolish Virgins from the original design (see page 158).

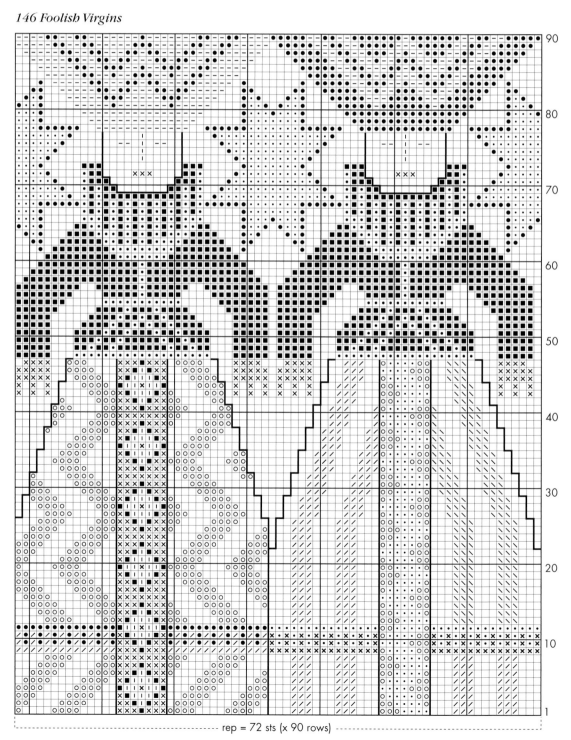

rep = 72 sts (x 90 rows)

147 Tropical Fish

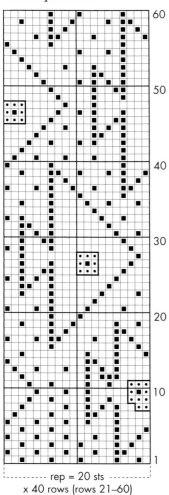

rep = 20 sts
x 40 rows (rows 21–60)

149 Heraldic Dogs

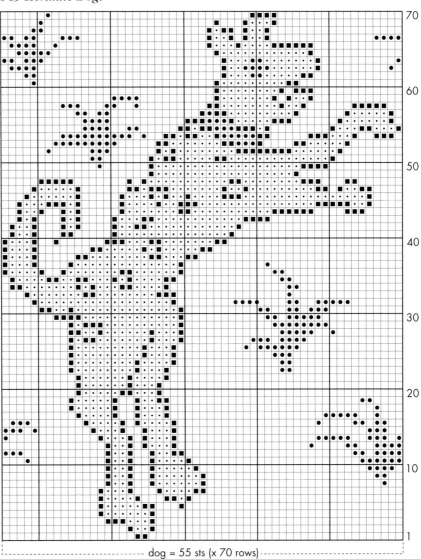

dog = 55 sts (x 70 rows)

148 Flamingoes

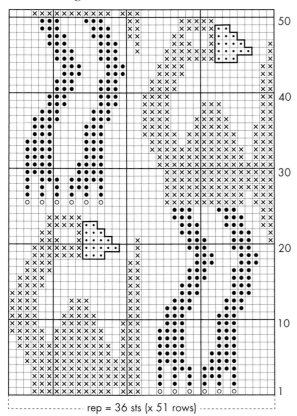

rep = 36 sts (x 51 rows)

147 Tropical Fish (page 61)

Modelled on an ancient Peruvian motif, this was originally designed as a machine knit for the Peruvian Connection catalogue. It is an easy and graphic knit.

148 Flamingoes (page 62)

Another Peruvian Connection knit sourced from an antique woven design, this could work well knit large in chunky yarns and a blues and greens palette.

149 Heraldic Dogs (page 62)

A witty and elegant Oriental hunting carpet was one of my sources for this knit covered with animated dogs.

Chart note: The chart gives only one of the several dogs on the original (see page 158). Use the motif singly or as a repeat on an all-over pattern.

150 Horses Brocade

150 Horses Brocade (page 63)

A large antique textile moved me to interpret this horse for a knit for Peruvian Connection, who featured it on a long coat surrounded with other motifs.

Chart note: Use the chart as a repeat for an all-over pattern or for a border. The horse could also be worked on its own without the foliage.

151 Cat (page 63)

A marquetry cat sat for this knit, which makes a good knitted cushion.

Chart note: To keep the cat lively, work a few closely toned stripes through its fur. The background can be anything you like – the original background is striped.

152 Leopard Skin (page 63)

Someone brought me an antique leopard pelt to knit from, and this stylized design was the result. Using three colours a row, it is easier to improvise this than to follow a chart.

Chart note: The chart gives a section of the original leopard pattern (see page 158). For a bigger piece of knitting, draw your own random shapes on a large piece of graph paper, or simply knit random shapes directly onto the needles and watch the pattern unfold.

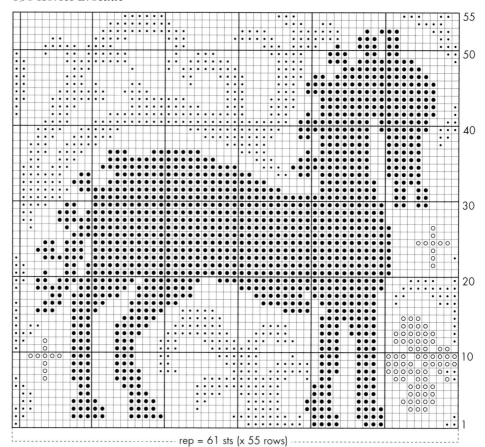

rep = 61 sts (x 55 rows)

152 Leopard Skin

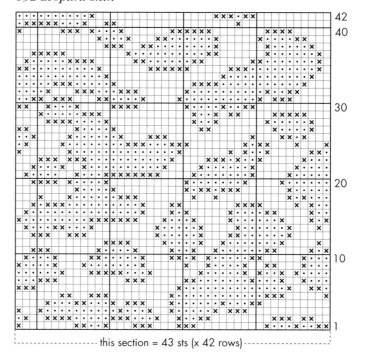

this section = 43 sts (x 42 rows)

151 Cat

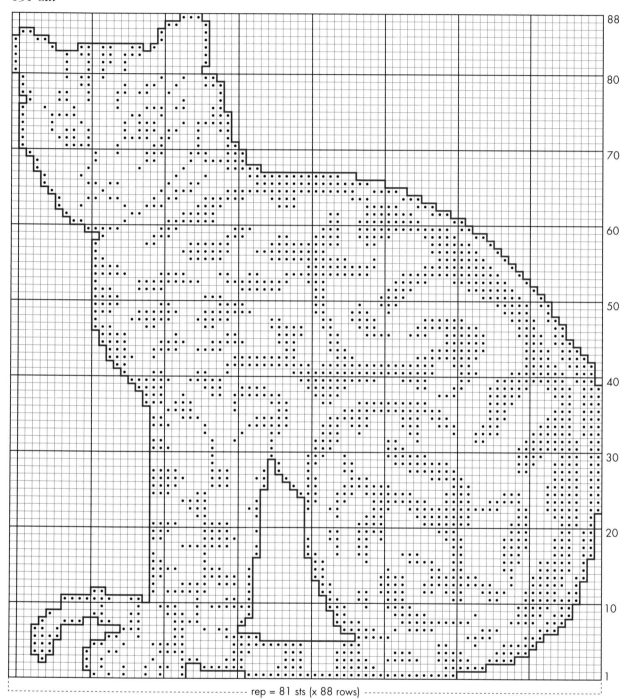

rep = 81 sts (x 88 rows)

153 Porcelain Patches CHART 1

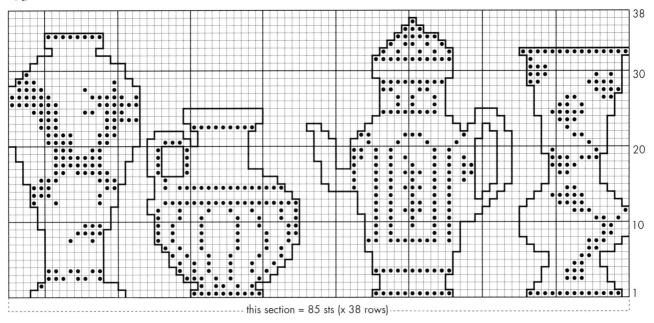

this section = 85 sts (x 38 rows)

153 Porcelain Patches CHART 2

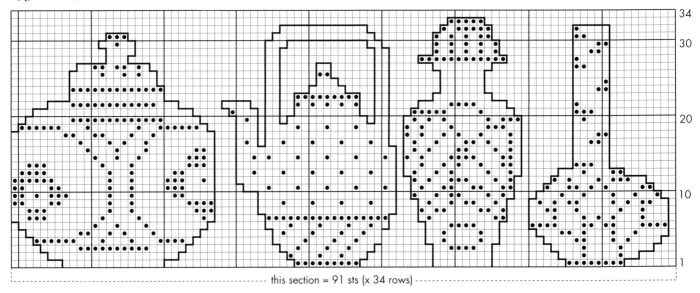

this section = 91 sts (x 34 rows)

pots

153 Porcelain Patches (page 64)

Oriental pots are one of my favourite themes. I have used them as the subjects on fabric design, knitting, patchwork, needlework, mosaic and, of course, in my still-life paintings. You can make this knit a lot more graphic by increasing the contrast – crisp blue-and-white pots on backgrounds of maroon, deep yellow or gunmetal grey.

Chart note: The chart gives a selection of the pots on the original design (see page 158). Work each pot inside a background rectangle 30 stitches wide and 40, 42, or 44 rows tall. Alternatively, work them in a row on a simple background as on design no. 155 (Blue and White Pots) on page 65.

154 Indian Pots on Shelves

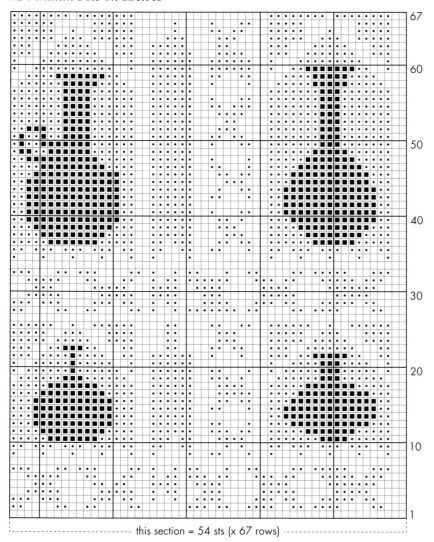

this section = 54 sts (x 67 rows)

154 Indian Pots on Shelves
(page 65)

Indian decorative arts often feature pot shapes. This dainty, graceful design was created for a cushion cover, but with more contrasting tones for a more intense effect it would make an excellent waistcoat/vest or child's jacket.

Chart note: The chart gives a section of the original cushion design (see page 158). It can be used as an all-over repeat, but be sure to change the pot colours and introduce a few stripes on some of the pots to animate the design.

155 Blue and White Pots
(page 65)

Use the chart for no. 153 (Porcelain Patches) for this design.

156 Apples

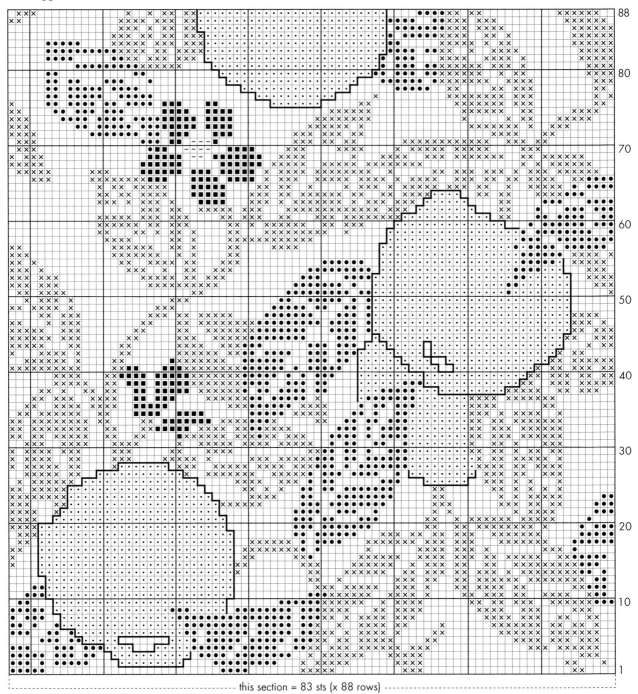

this section = 83 sts (x 88 rows)

fruits and foliage

156 Apples (page 66)

Taken off an old ceramic vase, this fruit theme makes a robust large brocade-like knit. The chart is big enough for a cushion cover.

Chart note: The apples are depicted with one symbol but should be shaded from dark to light as on the sample on page 66.

157 Bowls of Fruit

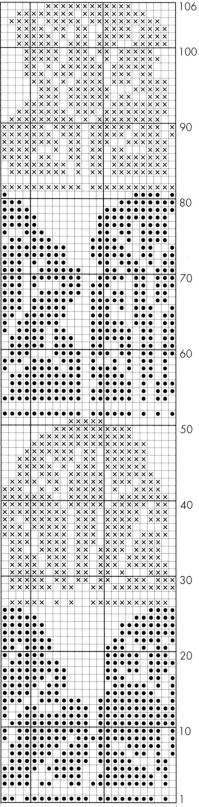

------ rep = 24 sts (x 32 rows) ------

158 Winter Trees

rep = 24 sts (x 106 rows)

157 Bowls of Fruit (page 66)

In the 70's I travelled through the Middle East and often saw decorations in shop windows of bowls full of pyramids of fruit, pickles or vegetables. This little design can be used as an all-over pattern, as it appeared on one of my women's jackets, or as a delicious border repeated sideways.

Chart note: If you like, vary the pattern on the blue-and-white bowls, working simple stripes or dots. Use the background colour for the fruit centres and background-diamond centres. Most of the rows (except for the rows with the bowls, which can be worked in intarsia) use only two colours.

158 Winter Trees (page 66)

This easy two-colours-a-row design was done as a machine knit for the Penny Plain Company. You could make the tree branches a third colour if you wish.

Chart note: Work the trees in subtle stripes of toning shades.

159 Overlapping Leaves

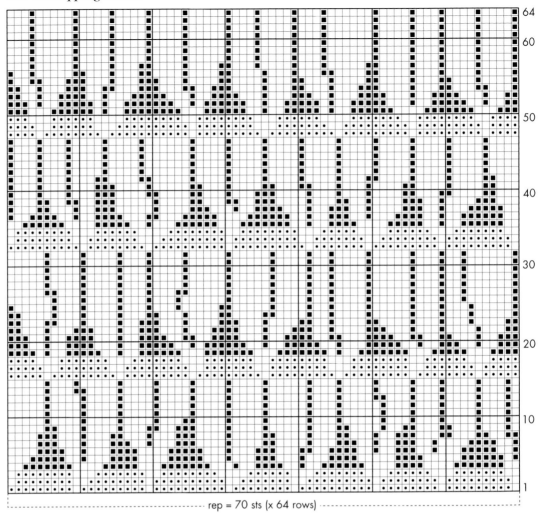

rep = 70 sts (x 64 rows)

161 Scroll Leaf

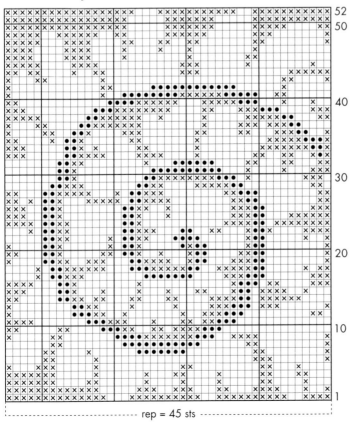

rep = 45 sts

162 Palm Trees

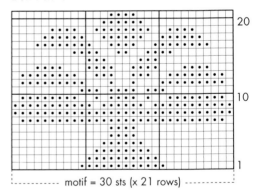

motif = 30 sts (x 21 rows)

130

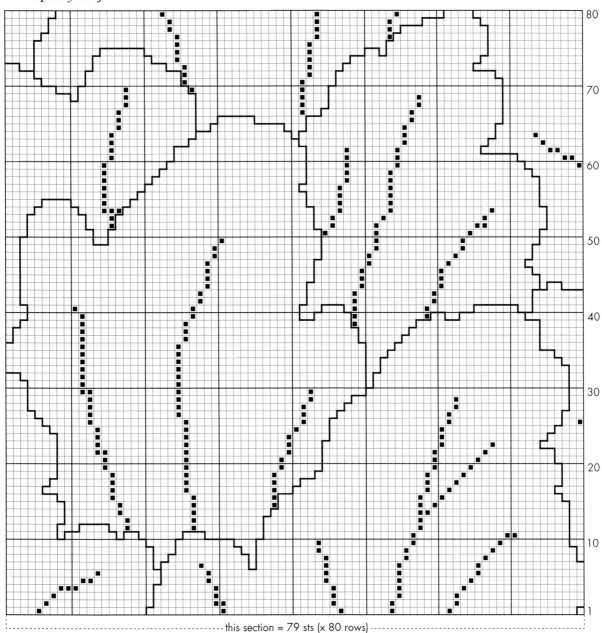

this section = 79 sts (x 80 rows)

159 Overlapping Leaves (page 67)

This really easy two-colours-a-row knit makes a nice starter pattern to get used to Fair Isle knitting. Great for scarves, as a border or in chunky yarns for a jacket.

Chart note: Each row of leaves starts with the one-stitch leaf tips in the gaps between the previous row of leaves. With this in mind you can improvise your own leaf shapes without having to look at a chart, and change their shapes all the way up your piece of knitting. Alternatively, just repeat chart rows 1–64, working each row of leaves in toning stripes that start light at the tips and get darker as they go up.

160 Tapestry Leaf (page 67)

One of my all-time classics, I designed this to go with a Liberty Print in the late 80's. Many people find this a surprisingly easy knit as you get large areas of each colour. Do try your own personal colours – how about a really bright autumn palette?

Chart note: The chart gives only a section of the original design (see page 158). If you want a bigger knit, take this section as your starting point and draw your own chart on graph paper with overlapping leaf shapes. Knit each leaf in a different set of toning shades, starting with dark tones at the bottom and ending with light tones at the top.

161 Scroll Leaf (page 67)

A detail from a fifteenth-century tapestry sparked off my imagination for this fern-like leaf shape. It makes an exciting border. Or, use it as a tile-like repeat, changing the background colour for each curled leaf.

162 Palm Trees (page 67)

I found a motif like this on a child's sweater in a Moroccan market. It makes a delightful child's coat and would be quite powerful in black and white.

Chart note: Arrange the motifs in staggered or stacked rows.

163 Daisy

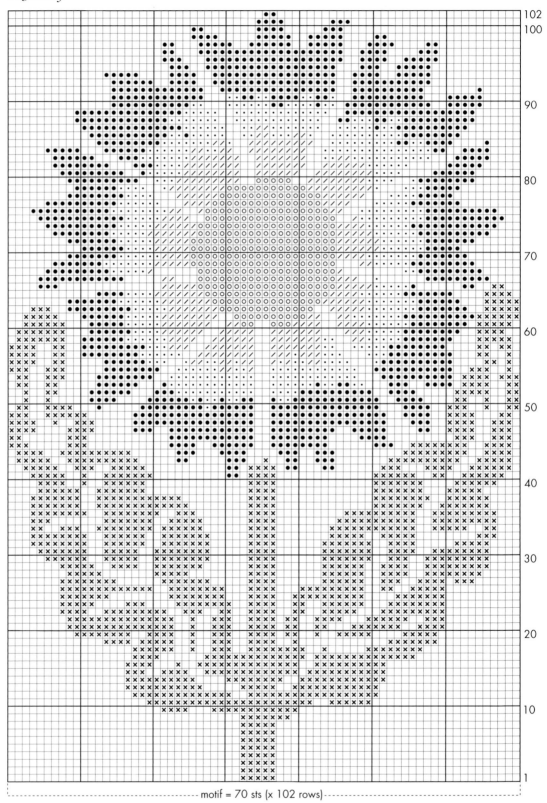

motif = 70 sts (x 102 rows)

164 Suzani Flower

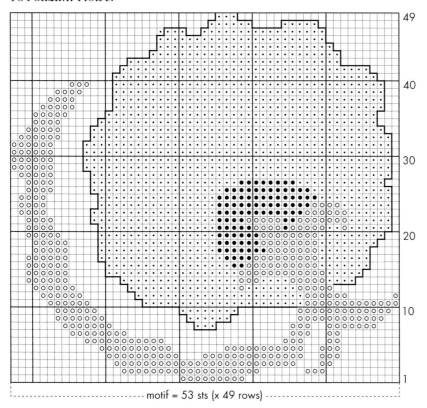

motif = 53 sts (x 49 rows)

165 Caucasian Flower

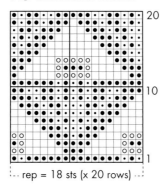

rep = 18 sts (x 20 rows)

flowers

163 Daisy (page 68)
Here's a brazen daisy for a child's sweater. I used it for a sock design, the centre of the daisy hitting the ankle-bone. You could try it as a repeating motif for a long stole.
Chart note: See sample on page 68 and design no. 194 on page 79 for colour ideas.

164 Suzani Flower (page 68)
Classic Middle Eastern suzani embroideries are packed with boldly delineated blooms like these. The embroideries are usually worked on off-white grounds so this is a departure from tradition. Try an even darker ground and brighter flowers if you want a vivid Spanish embroidered shawl look.
Chart note: The chart gives one motif from the original sweater design. Sprinkle the motifs over your knitting, occasionally flopping the image for the reverse shape (to do this, just read the odd-numbered rows as wrong-side rows instead of right-side). For more variety and movement, add a few of your own flower shapes that have similar but not exactly the same outlines.

165 Caucasian Flower (page 68)
This snappy stylized repeating flower was adapted from an old carpet where so many good knit patterns can be found.
Chart note: See the sample on page 68 for colour ideas.

166 Dangling Vine Flower

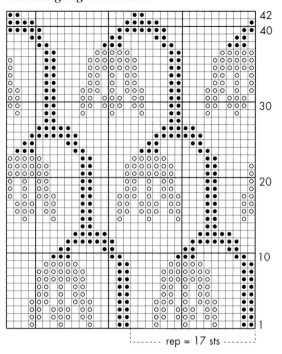

rep = 17 sts

166 Dangling Vine Flower
(page 69)

This robust brocade-like design can be used for an all-over pattern or as a deep border.

Chart note: The row repeat for this pattern is 289 rows long, so hopefully you will get the hang of it after row 42! Just move the flowers to the left five stitches with every fresh row of them. Use the intarsia technique for the stems, and work the rest of the row with just two colours – one for the flowers and one for the background.

167 Muriel's Tall Flowers
(page 69)

I designed this large-scale flower for my friend Muriel Latow, for a poncho-like coat worked in chunky yarns. Try it with finer yarns for a totally different look.

Chart note: The chart gives a section of the original design, but it can be used as an all-over pattern or border. To make the stems and leaves longer, first work rows 1–10, then repeat rows 9 and 10 over and over. When the stems are the desired length, work rows 11–66.

167 Muriel's Tall Flowers

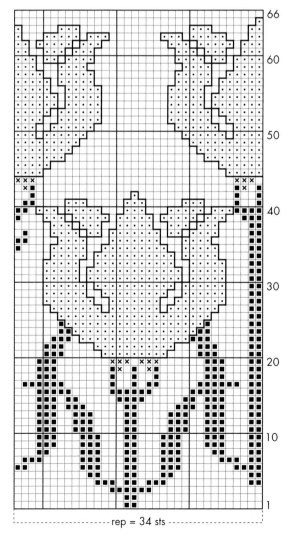

rep = 34 sts

168 Chrysanthemum

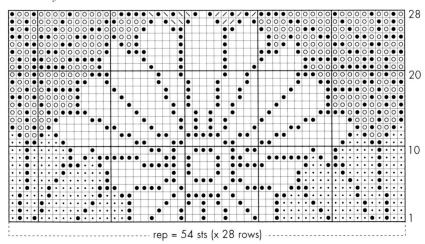

rep = 54 sts (x 28 rows)

169 Rows of Poppies

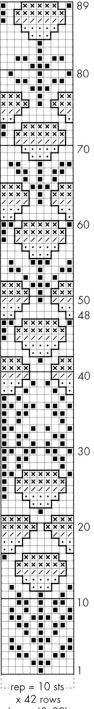

rep = 10 sts
x 42 rows
(rows 48–89)

170 Kaleidoscope

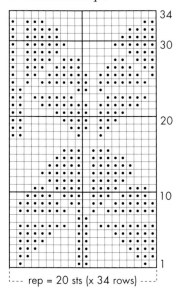

rep = 20 sts (x 34 rows)

168 Chrysanthemum (page 69)
Intrigued by Japanese formal pattern making, I found this dense brocade-style design a very satisfying knit. It could be knit up in so many moods – black, white and grey for a real change, or the colours of the Spanish Combs (design no. 182 on page 73).
Chart note: Work each flower in a different set of toning shades.

169 Rows of Poppies (page 69)
A fabric design on an Indian miniature painting was my source for these poppies. I look forward to seeing this as a lacy all-over pattern on a fine knit. The first 28 rows of the chart could make a lush border pattern for other designs.
Chart note: Although the majority of rows use only two colours, some use three.

170 Kaleidoscope (page 69)
When this appeared in the Woman and Home *magazine in Britain, it was an instant runaway success. Perhaps it's the two-colours-a-row ease of it. Do change the palette to suit.*
Chart note: Work the flowers and background in contrasting stripes, but for an easy knit, stick to only two colours a row – one for the background and one for the repeating motifs.

171 Turkish Carnation

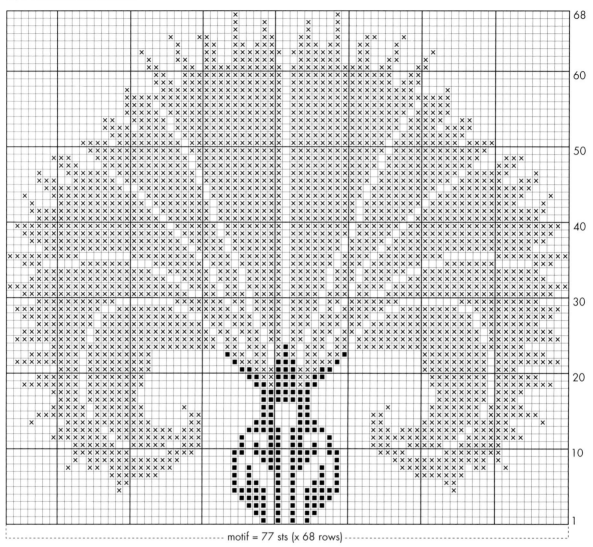

motif = 77 sts (x 68 rows)

171 Turkish Carnation

(page 70)

Long before I thought of doing my first book, Glorious Knitting, *I used these large blooms for a design in a book called* Creative Dressing *and it made such a stir that I was encouraged to do a book on my own. I've seen many colourways of this over the years and look forward to many more.*

Chart note: Position the motifs in stacked or staggered rows, tightly packed together.

172 Chinese Rose

172 Chinese Rose (page 70)
This candelabra of flowers was a great favourite with many knitters. It can be knit graphically in flat colours for contrast, or quite atmospheric in marls and tweedy tones. Although it looks complex, it is relatively easy to knit once you get in your stride.

173 Blanket Flower (page 70)
A woven blanket I saw in Peru had a brocade-like flower motif like this. I hope you enjoy its two-colours-a-row simplicity.

Chart note: For this design, use one set of closely toning shades for the leaves and another for the flowers.

173 Blanket Flower

rep = 57 sts (x 54 rows)

174 Exotic Bloom (page 70)
I've not used this on a garment, but am enchanted by the shape and boldness of it. It would be beautiful as a stole with Flower Ribbon borders (see design no. 181 on page 72).

175 Tropical Brocade (page 71)
An Oriental woven brocade fabric suggested this knit to me. It reminds me of my favourite island, Bali. Why not try working it in a rich silk and gold lurex for an evening top?

Chart note: The chart can also be knit from the side so the rows become the stitches (105-stitch repeat) and the stitches become the rows (70-row repeat).

174 Exotic Bloom

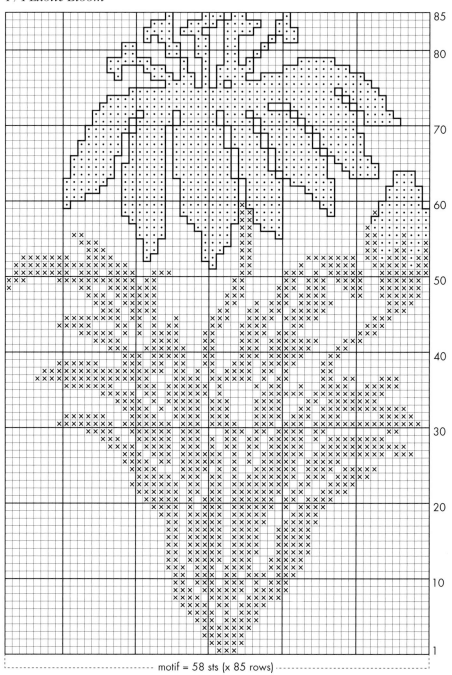

motif = 58 sts (x 85 rows)

175 Tropical Brocade

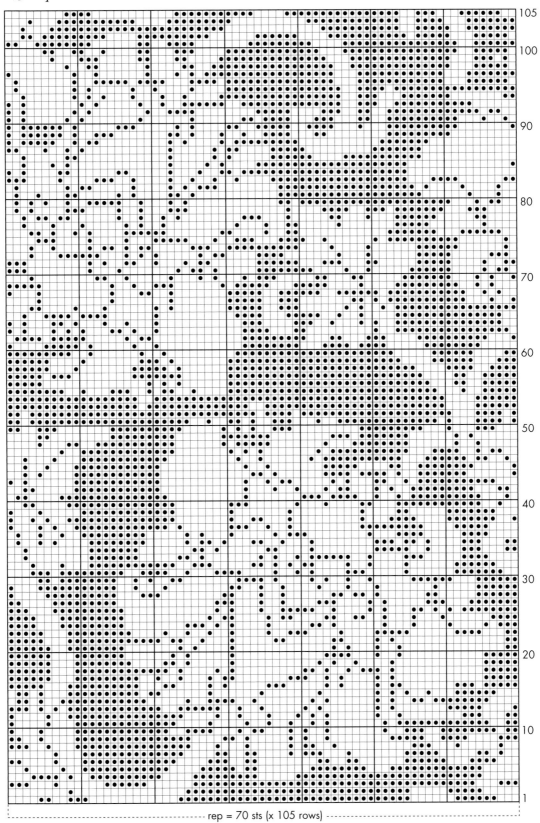

rep = 70 sts (x 105 rows)

176 Dark Daisy CHART 1

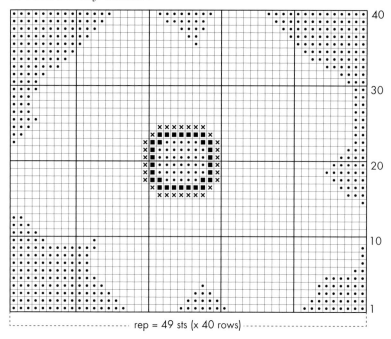

rep = 49 sts (x 40 rows)

176 Dark Daisy CHART 2

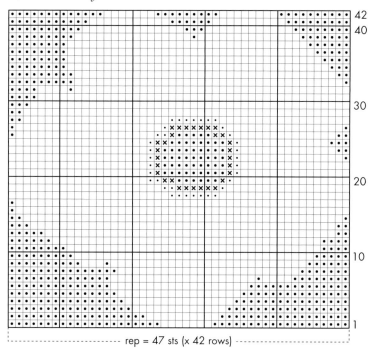

rep = 47 sts (x 42 rows)

179 Teeny Flower

motif =
7 sts
(x 7 rows)

177 Damask Flower

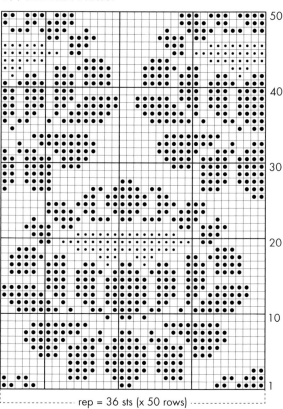

rep = 36 sts (x 50 rows)

176 Dark Daisy (page 71)
This simple design is probably one of the most wearable of my knitted flowers. It becomes very brocade-like in closely toned colours, but could, of course, look gorgeous in strong contrasts as well.
Chart note: The charts give two of the motifs from the original knit. Use them positioned as you choose on your knit or make up your own similar random shapes on a big combined chart.

177 Damask Flower (page 72)
Playful, bright colours bring this opulent brocade-like pattern to life. It can be knit in so many different colour combos, even black and white.

178 Damask Flower (page 72)
Use the chart for no. 177 (Damask Flower) for this design.

179 Teeny Flower (page 72)
Set this motif inside vertical or horizontal stripes to make simple, smart borders (see page 150).
Chart note: Stagger or stack the flower motifs for repeating rows.

180 Cheviot Gardens

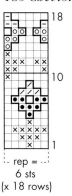

rep =
6 sts
(x 18 rows)

181 Flower Ribbon

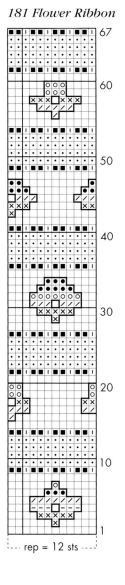

rep = 12 sts

182 Spanish Combs

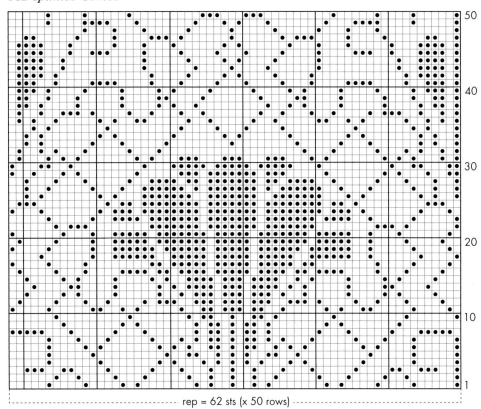

rep = 62 sts (x 50 rows)

183 Lattice Flower

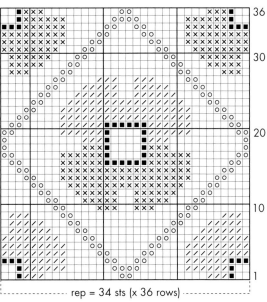

rep = 34 sts (x 36 rows)

180 Cheviot Gardens (page 72)
Chart note: This is an easy two-colours-a-row pattern. Keep changing the flower colours to add variety.

181 Flower Ribbon (page 72)
The fabulous row upon row of embroidered ribbons on Slavic dance costumes sparked off the idea for these swathes of pansies. Use it as an all-over pattern or a border. I'd like to see someone combine this and all the other border patterns in the book as a long coat with nothing but borders all the way up.
Chart note: Many of the rows use only one colour and the others only two colours, so this is an easy knit.

182 Spanish Combs (page 73)
Taken from a Japanese brocade, this is one of my personal favourites. I look forward to seeing it in lots of different colourings.
Chart note: Keep the outline colour the same throughout, but work each flower in a different set of toning shades.

183 Lattice Flower (page 74)
Chart note: Work the flower centres in the background colour. Use different colours for each flower.

184 Tulips (page 74)

I haven't designed many realistic flowers in knitting, but I am fond of this jaunty colourful idea. A black ground with earthy tones for the tulips could be attractive, or light and spring-like with a pink or pale green ground.

Chart note: The chart gives two of the tulips from the original design to create a repeat for a repeating all-over design. Use different colours for each flowerhead.

185 Turkish Carnation (page 75)

Use the chart for no. 171 (Turkish Carnation) on page 136 for this design.

186 Box Flower (page 75)

This strong ethnic flower idea makes a good border motif.

Chart note: The design uses no more than three colours a row.

187 Paisley Stripes (page 76)

Use this as a charming deep border or endlessly repeated up a scarf, garment or cushion cover.

Chart note: This pattern is mostly two colours a row, with a few one-colour rows.

184 Tulips

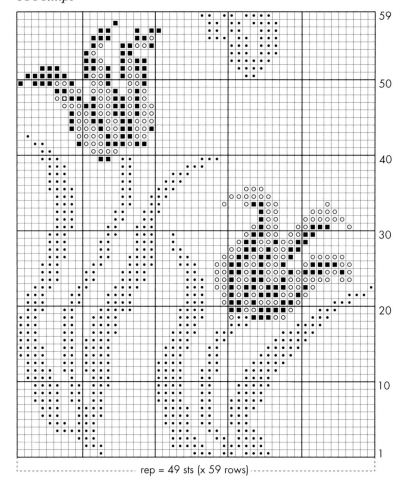

rep = 49 sts (x 59 rows)

187 Paisley Stripes

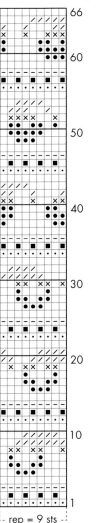

rep = 9 sts
(x 66 rows)

186 Box Flower

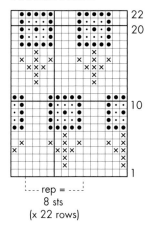

rep =
8 sts
(x 22 rows)

188 Patch Flower

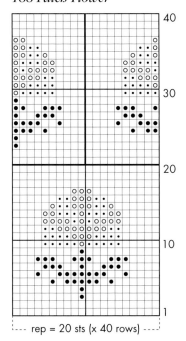

rep = 20 sts (x 40 rows)

188 Patch Flower (pages 76–77)
A woven Indian cloth provided this idea. Try it as an unaffected all-over pattern and add a rich border, possibly the Paisley Stripes (see design no. 187 on page 76).
Chart note: Change the background and flower colours in each square, using the intarsia technique.

189 Damask Flower (page 77)
Use the chart for no. 177 (Damask Flower) on page 140 for this design.

190 Big Damask Flower (page 78)
This massive bloom that graced the back and front of a long cardigan in my book Glorious Knitting *has been knitted by people all over the world in wildly different colourways. Just be sure to put glorious tones in the centre of the flower.*

190 Big Damask Flower

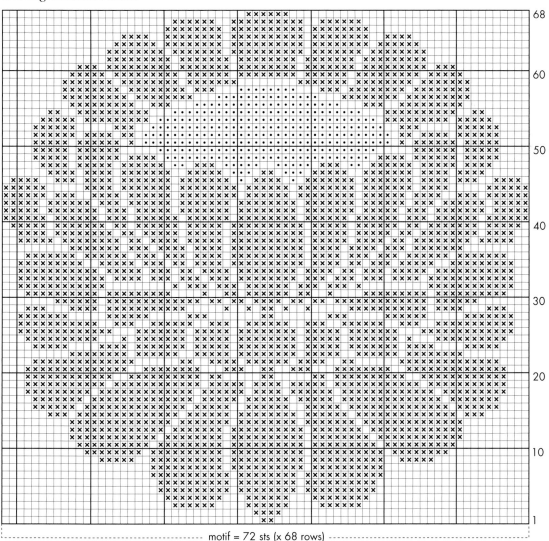

motif = 72 sts (x 68 rows)

143

191 Paisley

rep = 84 sts (x 103 rows)

192 Papyrus

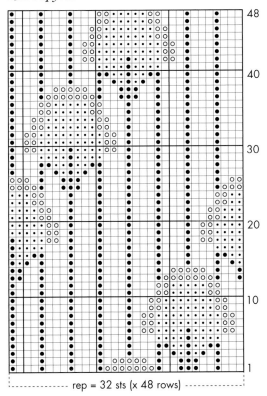

48
40
30
20
10
1

---------- rep = 32 sts (x 48 rows) ----------

193 Monotone Roses

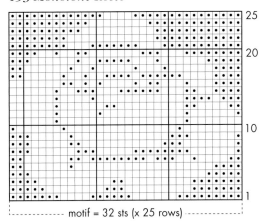

25
20
10
1

---------- motif = 32 sts (x 25 rows) ----------

195 Wildflower

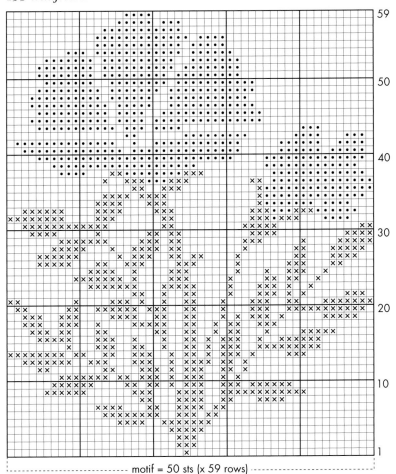

59
50
40
30
20
10
1

---------- motif = 50 sts (x 59 rows) ----------

191 Paisley (page 79)

Although the subdued colour scheme is quite effective, I'd rather see this paisley done in a myriad of pastels, or even with quite sharp colours on a vivid coloured ground – black, red or hot pumpkin orange – as the Indians might do.

Chart note: Reverse the shape if desired, by reading the odd-numbered rows as the wrong side instead of the right side.

192 Papyrus (page 79)

Egyptian painting is intriguing, especially the way flowers or animals are made into very stylized forms yet retain their essence. This is a knit interpretation of my own.

193 Monotone Roses (page 79)

I designed this flower for the Scottish fashion designer Bill Gibb in the 80's when roses were having one of their periodic comebacks. It never got used but I still like it, so here it is for you to play with. Why not try it on socks, sweaters or cushions.

194 Daisy (page 79)

Use the chart for no. 163 (Daisy) on page 132 for this design.

195 Wildflower (page 79)

This motif was designed for a baby blanket in cottons for the American Vogue Knitting magazine. The delicate leafy spray could be staggered all over a knit, worked in rows for a deep border or used as a single detail on a cushion cover.

Chart note: Work toning stripes through the flowers.

145

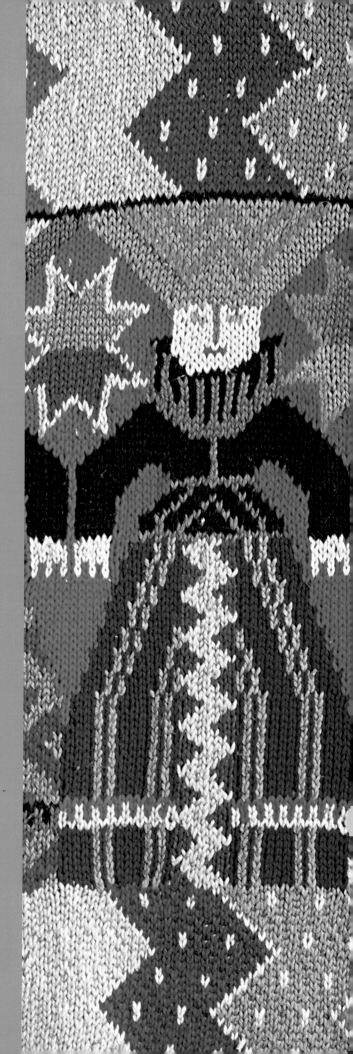

using the charts

My collection of knitting motifs and patterns was put together to spark off your imagination and draw you into the enjoyable art of colour knitting. To start you on your way, here are some helpful hints on how to use the charts for your own knitted pieces. Approaching design, knitting from charts, choosing colours and textures, and mixing patterns are all covered. And most important of all, you will find illustrated instructions and tips for the simple techniques used for colourwork knitting.

approaching design

Designing multicoloured knitting isn't as mystifying as it may seem at first glance. You could use any of the charts in the book and introduce your own personal colours for your first attempt at originality. Or, you could mix or adapt the charts to suit your imagination. There's also nothing stopping you from making up a unique pattern or motif. The task of designing is really quite straightforward if you take it step by step.

When I receive a commission to design a collection, I usually receive a sample card of the yarn colours that are available for that season. I send for a ball of each colour that I fancy and spread them out before me, letting my mind roam across the colours to see if any general idea is sparked by this particular range. Then I go to my vast collection of source books – books on textiles of all sorts, carpets to dress prints, but even more useful, books on decorated surfaces like wall tiles, mosaics, pottery, beaded bags or fans. Any of these sources might reveal an idea that seems exciting for my chosen colours.

Next, I take some graph paper and draw out the motif that caught my eye – as you know, each tick or symbol in a square on the graph paper will become a stitch of knitting. I merely outline the particular shape on the paper; the intricate shading in of the motif is done during the knitting process. Sometimes a few of the colour differences are drawn in on my original charts just to indicate colour contrasts, for example between different parts of a motif or between an outline and a motif, but there's no need to draw out all the colour changes (see two of my own charts below). It's better to introduce new colours as the knitting progresses when you can see how they really work next to each other.

The secret to making graphed knitting charts is to pick motifs or subjects that have shapes that are bold but fairly simple. For example, single flowers rather than multi-petaled double ones – objects, in other words, that have a clear, readable silhouette. Once you have the outline, while knitting you can imbue the shape with as much colour as you like, a contrast centre to a poppy or just a warm blush of tone in ombré shading.

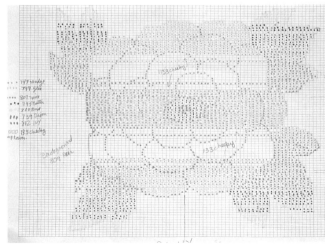

working with chart patterns

Following a knitting chart is perfectly easy once you get used to it. I cover everything above the line of knitting I am working on at that moment. All of my designs are worked in stocking (stockinette) stitch, so you knit from right to left on your knit row and read the chart in the same direction. On the purl rows (the even-numbered rows) you read the chart from left to right. As with knitting, you start at the bottom of the chart (row 1, a knit row) and work upwards.

Many of my charted flowers and fruits have a simple two-colours-a-row format, as this is the easiest colour knitting technique. For richer effects, you should always feel free to add extra colours in a row, but I think you will find that these simple two-colours-a-row images are quite effective. It's all too easy to get bogged down trying to

follow a chart when there are too many colour changes in the row, especially if there are only a few stitches of each colour close together. (See pages 156–157 for the simple colourwork methods you can use.)

Several of my charts have only one motif. To use these motifs for an all-over pattern, just repeat the motif across your knitting leaving a gap between the shapes. The following line of motifs can be placed directly above the first – this gives a formal, solid feel to the pattern. For a more organic, natural flow, you can stagger the motifs by placing the next row of motifs so they sit between those of the previous rows motif. Scatter the motifs for an even more random look.

Knitting from a chart doesn't mean you always have to look at the chart for every single stitch. On simple charts, once you get going you never have to look at the chart again after you've done the first pattern repeat because it's so easy to remember. My favourite knitting when I am in a hurry or travelling is to memorize a simple geometric like Tumbling Blocks (see chart on page 96), Small Steps (see above and charts on page 101) or Persian Poppy (see chart on page 117), make a selection of colours and just knit away. This way I can concentrate solely on the colour harmonies and not have the inconvenience of making sense of a chart.

what to make with the charts

There are any number of things you can make with the patterns in this book and you're sure to come up with your own ideas for using them to suit your knitting ability. But if you're stuck for a starting point, here are a few things you could consider attempting to knit.

If you have never tried Fair Isle or two-colours-a-row knitting, you might want to start out by playing with colour in simple, one-colour-at-a-time stripes. Why not take all the stripes of that nature in the book and make a delicious changing stripe sweater. Make the sweater pieces out of simple rectangles and use a group of colours (light or dark) that work together. You could do the back, front and each sleeve in a completely different set of stripes for a very young and spirited pullover.

A good first Fair Isle project would be a sampler scarf. Take at least three small repeating patterns (see pages 18 and 19 for example) and knit those in the first dozen or so rows of the scarf to form a border. Then take a sequence of all over geometrics like Tumbling Blocks (no. 64 on page 28), followed by stars (see pages 44–47), followed by Persian Poppy (no. 135 on page 52), then mirror the image back through this sequence, ending with a repeat of the initial border pattern. You could also do this with a sequence of motifs from the figurative chapter to wonderful effect.

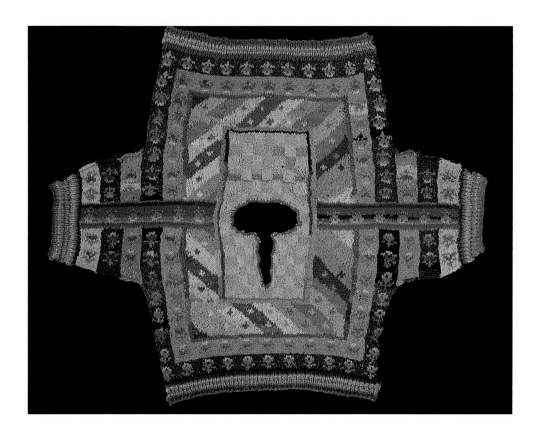

A cushion is another excellent trial item – knit a square of one big flower or several smaller ones, then make a mitred border on all four sides using a small pattern repeat.

The perfect small project is a child's sweater. Make it very personal and quite magical by using several borders and motifs from each of the chapters. I knit little garments all in one piece (see opposite page). You can start and finish one or two on a holiday. Simply pack a supply bag containing a bouquet of coloured yarns of matching thickness, your pattern source book and your imagination – I do some of my most inspired work away from the studio in this way. It's a wonderful antidote to long delays in travel these days.

For a simple hat, first knit a band of Fair Isle 2 or 3 inches (5–7.5cm) wide that fits around the head. Then crochet round and round to complete the top, and add another row or two of crochet around the bottom to firm up the shape – quick and effective.

When you have put your toe in the water of colour knitting you will either be running smartly back to your cables in one colour or be excited to try large multicoloured projects. As I assembled my swatch collection my fingers started itching. I wanted to sit down and start combining these motifs in unusual ways. I dreamed of making a big patchwork bedcover using all the various flower prints in the book. The backgrounds could be kept one unifying colour or many shades of a colour – say red, magenta, orange, scarlet, crimson or soft sugared almond pastel; or a dark mood with black, maroon, teal blue or peat brown. I once saw a stunning tablecloth made from patches of old flower prints with black backgrounds that an artist had collected at charity shops – lots of different-scale prints with the black backgrounds unifying the hodgepodge of fabrics.

A blanket of knitted patches, whether of simple stripes or more complex motifs, could be a great knit project for a group – like the old quilting bees. You could make small or large throws for charity from everybody's swatches. By crocheting around each contribution you needn't worry about the various tensions not coming up with a uniform size, just add more border until they equal out. Tassels or fringes could be a luxurious finish to your splendid group effort.

In our family all the knitters contribute a square of colourwork knitting to a baby blanket for the newest arrival. My sister Holly skilfully combines the swatches with colourful crochet to make family heirlooms.

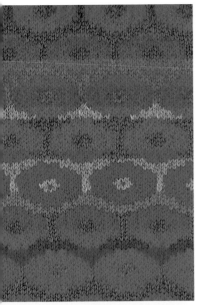

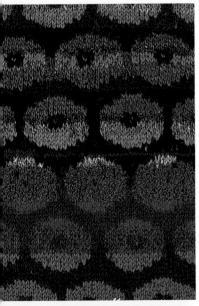

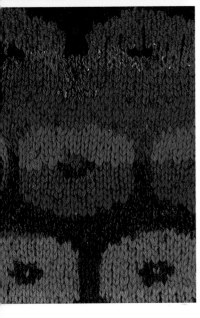

choosing colour palettes

Working out a new colour scheme can be quite a mysterious and daunting process, or the most natural happening in the world. If you have a carpet you want to match a cushion with, or a patterned skirt you want to match with a sweater, the solution is pretty obvious and fun, capturing the same colour mood as the starting point.

One of the ways I play with pattern and colour is to knit swatches of a new motif or pattern in at least three or four colour combinations or 'colourways'. Each swatch is just one repeat of the motif or several if it is small-scale. These colour trials need never go to waste. At a later date you can join them together into a 'sampler' blanket like I do – at the very least you'll eventually have enough for a patchwork cushion.

The main thing is to have a go at trying out colours, the wilder the better. None of us designers really know what works until we see it, so sampling becomes wonderfully exciting as you stumble on really unpredictable and interesting colourings. The many versions of my Persian Poppy (left and right) give just a taste of how many effective colourways can be created for a single simple charted design (see chart on page 117).

If you have a hard time starting on this exciting colour play, choose a postcard of a painting that has colour combinations that make your pulse work faster. Then select colours in the painting and try to use them in the same ratio as they are in that artwork. For instance, if it's a mainly blue painting with just a shot of orange in one small object, choose a lot of shades of blue and use only a small accent of orange in your knit.

Many yarn shops help these days by displaying their various yarns in colour groupings. You can see at a glance how magenta and orange make red really dance, but often a bit of emerald or turquoise will spike up that red. Multiple shades of similar colours are a definite rich way to proceed, but do find a 'kick' colour as all one colour family, even with 20 or 30 tones, can look strangely dull after all your work. This 'kick' can be very subtle. All it takes to make a scheme of many tones of beige hum is a whisper of lavender or grey green. All yellows often need is a touch of sky blue or apple green.

Contrast of dark and light tones is definitely a tricky area – too much contrast and the work looks cheap and coarse, not enough and motifs dissolve into minestrone soup! For example, a multi-toned ground needs to contrast enough from the foreground motifs for the motif shapes to read clearly – you don't want a mush of tone with motifs indistinct from the background. (Though a little mushiness could be handy in a charming old faded antique colour scheme!) I often go for low contrast in

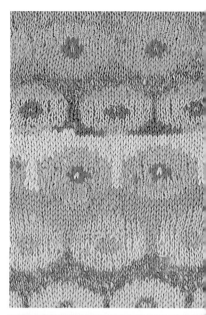

my fabric prints, patchworks and knit designs. I like the vibration of many close tones mingling together. But for drama and bold statements, high contrast can be just the ticket. If you have large areas of each colour a closer tonal value can still sing out. On the other hand, small fractured designs need more edge to read. But do notice what a deep glow you get from the shades of the same or similar colours together. Think of marquetry woodwork on old furniture – those rich ambers, ochres, rusty wood tones, and ebony for delineation.

Whatever your palette, be sure to put the effort into those colour trial swatches. I was once shown a knit that looked like a jazzy Harris tweed. 'It's a teapot,' said the proud creator. For the life of me I couldn't make out what all her efforts had rendered.

For colour combos that work, a walk through a decorative arts museum or a shop full of antiques or fashion prints can educate your eye as to what works and is alive and unusual. Even builders' yards with stacked bricks or wood can give you wonderful tonal ideas. Believe it or not, I designed Floating Circles (no. 131 on page 50) from a black tray of eyeshadow I saw in a TV makeup studio. For subtle combos, study stone walls, stones on a beach, or dried leaves on the street in late autumn. For slightly higher colouring, study Oriental porcelains, painters like Vuillard, or the watercolours of Beatrix Potter. For outrageous, dancing-on-the-table colour, look at *The Simpsons* cartoon on TV, circus and bullfighting posters, paintings by Emile Nolde, Matisse, or any of the Fauve school of painters. Or better still, travel to India, Africa or Guatemala and spend time in local markets.

Keep in mind that scale has a lot to do with the success or not of various patterns. Sometimes large areas of dullish colour become quite strong because of the mass, whereas a tiny dab of colour on a motif has to be pretty intense to read.

You can unify a colour palette by knitting with two or three strands of yarn together, keeping one of the strands the same colour and changing the others. For bright pastels, you might run a silvery grey along with the colours to create a pearly effect, or black along with deep jewel tones to deepen and slightly merge them.

Hard, clean white rarely appears in my designs, but in case you feel that's sounding like a rule, there are times when a really fresh, harsh white is just what's needed. You will notice that I often suggest a motif would be good in black and white because it has such a good silhouette. Also, have some fun seeing how utterly changed a design that was done in pastels, say, can be when knit in strong colours against black.

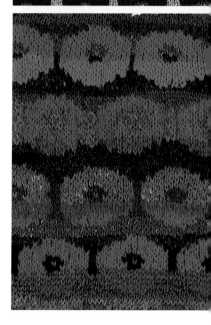

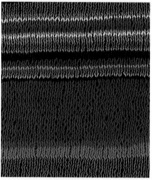

working with texture

These days yarn shops are spilling over with textured yarns, man-made or natural, containing elements of feathers, ribbons, lurex, mohair, silk, slubs and even sequins. Since I usually have my eye more in the past, I find all the glitz and glitter a little tinsely. During one whole period I used lurex but tried to make it feel like old Byzantine churches and ecclesiastical robes.

Mohair used judiciously with chenille can give great depth and quality to reds (see Big Circles; no. 136 on pages 52–53) or a rich deep brown palette. Silk, linen and mercerized cotton can give highlights to a pale palette. Running several different colours of yarns together to create marls can be an exciting way to make a bulky blanket or large-scale coat. If one of these is mohair it lightens the weight of it all.

Textured yarns (mohair and chenille) can be seen in the top two swatches on the right. The Houses swatches worked in chunky yarn and in a medium-weight yarn show how yarn thickness also effects the textural look of your knitting.

Although I've not tried much embroidery on knitting, I've seen it done wonderfully. Cross stitch, chain stitch or running stitches for big flower bursts, or dainty daisy-like repeats around a waistcoat or child's jacket would provide an attractive change of texture.

I haven't yet mastered textural stitches like cables and bobble stitches, as plain old stocking (stockinette) stitch has been enough for me, allowing me to concentrate on colour. Reverse stocking stitch is my one departure as you can see on page 12 (design no. 7) – this is a very effective way to add texture to a plain stripe.

Please do experiment, as I'm sure you will, with all sorts of textural stitches on these motifs or in the backgrounds. It will add another exciting note to your knitting.

mixing patterns

All these diverse designs under one cover should encourage some creative mixtures of motifs. Flowers and stars, animals and fruits, and borders with everything, make for rich designs. Lots of borders grouped together is really lively. Even rows of animals or flowers make good borders – you can add a contrast stripe behind the motifs to make them more borderlike. Certainly in the same garment you can mix patterns. Think of all the trendy T-shirts with odd sleeves, and a different front and back. I've often paired a strongly patterned waistcoast/vest front with a striped back that echoes colours of the front (see right and opposite page top). During an early lecture on my

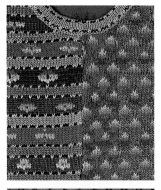

work, I showed a slide of one of my patterned waistcoats with a striped back and a woman yelled from the audience, 'You could have got the back and front to match if you had really tried!' And there I was thinking I had achieved a really biblical look!

Many of my heavily patterned garments have striped ribbing at the bottom and on the sleeves and neck to keep the colour story flowing, instead of abruptly ending with a big solid-colour rib (see right). As a general rule, I use the medium to darker tones of the garment colours in my ribbing. On a darkish garment a light bright colour in the rib would grab too much attention.

Some of my borders are shown here to inspire, but fresh ideas for combining patterns are always coming to me. I've long been an admirer of a type of paisley design that is laid out in stripes of different colours with small motifs running through them. The simple row-upon-row elegance of these coloured sections could be achieved by knitting similar-sized borders, one after another, right up a shawl or long waistcoat or done vertically on a wide coat. This could easily be knitted by starting at the cuff and knitting across the garment, so the knitting is sideways on.

To knit a delicious mix of patterns, take the layout of Contrast Stripe Patch (no. 79 on page 32) and do each patch as a flower print from the book. For colouring, you could choose many shades of ochre or blue, or whatever colour mood you wanted the end product to reflect.

An Eastern way of using pattern is to do a carpet-type composition, with very detailed decorative borders of flowers or animals surrounding a centre in some form of stripe. Wouldn't that be quite smart for a jacket or coat – a lush border of large and small flowers or animals with a bold stripe in any of the ones on offer here?

Why not pick up those needles and do a series of cushion-size swatches to try out different motif combos and colourways. You'll be surprised how easy it is to get hooked on the excitement of seeing them come to life.

colour knitting techniques

Knitting with lots of colours is much easier than it looks. If you already have a grasp of the knitting basics – casting on, knit, purl and casting/binding off – you'll be able to work with masses of colours in no time at all. The tips I cover here show you how to introduce new colours and how to keep the ends from tangling. If you haven't ever attempted colour knitting, take the time to try out the methods that follow, using one of the simple charts in the library. And if you haven't picked up your needles for a while, read the tips carefully to remind yourself of the various colourwork techniques.

multicoloured knitting

Even an average knitter can learn how to work with a large number of colours, though it may seem an unsurmontable task at first. The easiest way to add lots of colours to your knitting is to stick to designs that use only two colours in a row. This technique is perfect for beginners. All you need to do is choose a design that has only a background colour and a motif colour in each row. Many of my charted desins are like this, for example Overlapping Leaves (no. 159 on page 67) or Flower Ribbon (no. 181 on page 72). Start out with two colours in your first row, one for the background and one for the motif. As your knitting progresses you can break off and change the background colour or the motif colour as often as you like, but you will only ever have two colours at once hanging at the back of the work.

Once you have mastered this simple way of adding lots of colour, you can try using more than two colours across your row. To avoid a never-ending tangle of yarn ends, just use short lengths 60–100cm/2–3ft long and add more lengths as they are needed. As the yarns tangle, simply pull through the colour you want to use next. It's as easy as that. If you only ever use 'manageable lengths' there is no end to the number of colours you can have on the go at once.

fair isle knitting

There are two basic methods for colourwork knitting. One is called the Fair Isle technique and it is used when two or more colours are used repeatedly across an entire row of knitting. The yarn not being used at any one time is carried across the wrong side of the work until it is needed again.

If only a few stitches are spanned by an unused yarn during Fair Isle knitting, it can simply be 'stranded' loosely across the back (see above).

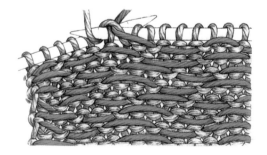

When there are more than about five stitches to span before the yarn is used again, it should be woven under and over the working yarn as you proceed (see above), so the loose strand is caught into the back of the knitting. This is called 'weaving in' or 'knitting-in'. Some knitters like to knit-in on every other stitch, but I find it sufficient to do it on every third stitch or so.

Another useful tip I usually give to knitters trying out the Fair Isle technique is to work stranding and weaving-in with a loose and relaxed tension on the stitches. If you pull the yarns too tightly, your knitting will pucker and you won't get the smooth surface you are aiming for. It helps to spread out the stitches to their correct width a few times in each row to keep them elastic.

intarsia knitting

The other technique for multicoloured knitting is called intarsia. This method is used when there are lots of different colours in a row, but each one is only used in an isolated area and not across the entire row. The yarn can simply be worked where it is needed and then left to hang at the back until it is reached again on the next row.

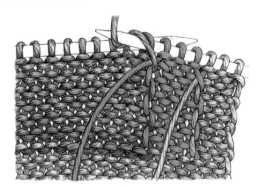

Where the colour change occurs in intarsia knitting, twist the two yarns together to avoid holes (see above). In many of my knitting designs, I use both the Fair Isle and intarsia techniques on the same piece of knitting. Any colour that is used across the entire row is worked in with the Fair Isle technique, and any colour needed in just one area in the intarsia method.

knitting-in yarn ends

This last tip is probably the one you'll be the most grateful for if you don't already know about it! To save hours of laborious work darning-in yarn ends when your knitting is completed, weave in all the ends as the knitting progresses. The technique for doing this is basically the same as for knitting-in the loose strands or 'floats' in Fair Isle knitting.

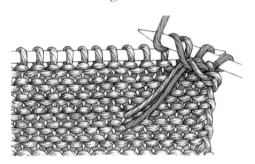

Each time you join in a new colour, leave about 8cm/3in extra on the end of both the old and new yarns, then knit the next two stitches with the new yarn. Holding both ends of yarn in your left hand, lay them over the working yarn and work the next stitch (see above).

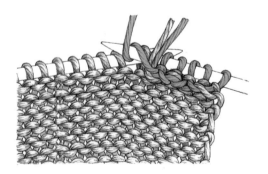

Now insert the right-hand needle into the next stitch in the usual way, bring the ends up behind the working yarn and work the next stitch. Carry on in this way, weaving the ends over and under the working yarn until they are completely knitted-in. If you are introducing a new colour but not finishing off the old colour, weave-in only the end of the new yarn.

chart sources

In order to have as many designs as possible to choose from in this book, only a section of some of the patterns have been charted. This is usually because the pattern does not break down into a simple repeat; instead the motifs or patterns vary in shape across the entire garment, cushion or blanket.

The following knits are some of those that have charts in this book showing only a section of the full design, but which have been charted in full in previous Kaffe Fassett books. They are given here for your reference, with their design number and the name of the original Kaffe Fassett book they first appeared in, where there is a full chart.

47 Little Boxes – page 24 (cushion cover), *Glorious Interiors*

58 Ribbon Design – page 111 (adult V-neck) and page 115 (child's V-neck), *Glorious Knitting*

82 Red Patch – page 127 (adult cardigan), *Glorious Knitting*

127 Geometric Star – page 58 (adult jacket), *Kaffe Fassett at the V&A* (UK), *Glorious Color* (US)

146 Foolish Virgins – pages 118–119 (adult jacket or crewneck), *Kaffe's Classics*

149 Heraldic Dogs – pages 84–86 (adult crewneck), *Kaffe's Classics*

152 Leopard Skin – pages 102–103, *Kaffe's Classics*

153 Porcelain Patches – pages 148–149 and 150–151 (adult coat), *Kaffe Fassett at the V&A* (UK), *Glorious Color* (US)

154 Indian Pots on Shelves – pages 96–97 (cushion cover), *Glorious Interiors*

160 Tapestry Leaf – pages 56–57 (adult crewneck), *Kaffe's Classics*

acknowledgments

Thanks firstly to all those many named and unnamed artists and craftsmen whose work has filled me with inspiration for these motifs.

Thanks to all my knitters over the years, especially Zoe Hunt, Jules Yeo, Maria Brennan, Kay Kettles, Franchesca Nurse and Charlotte Gunningleg, and to the knitters who have dared attempt my designs and the long-suffering yarn shops who have encouraged them.

Thanks most especially to the fantastic team who make my life run smoothly and allow me space and time to create – Richard Womersley, Belinda Mably, and above and beyond the call of duty Brandon Mably, who not only runs the show but found storage room for all the swatches in this book and more.

Thanks again to editor Sally Harding, to photographers Jon Stewart and Debbie Patterson, to Christine Wood who styled our book so elegantly, and to Grace Cheetham and Denise Bates at Ebury.

Thanks lastly to Rowan Yarns, the late Bill Gibb, *Vogue Knitting* and Peruvian Connection.